T0328081

BRITISH RECORD SHOP BAGS
1940s – 1990s

JONNY TRUNK

FUEL

FOREWORD

JON SAVAGE

These mostly square-shaped slivers of paper and plastic are artefacts from a lost age: a music economy based on physical objects that could only be bought, in person, from physical outlets. In the first thirty or forty years of British pop culture, the shop was the place: the agora, the arena where committed fans and casual buyers would meet and spend time, perhaps even talk to each other or hear something they might not previously have known. How many times have you bought something you first heard playing in a shop?

These brightly coloured objects are pure ephemera, designed only to carry the record inside from shop to home, from cash point to turntable. They were not meant to last, nor would they have done without Jonny Trunk's prescient salvage. From the perspective of the 21st century, they comprise an alternative history of British pop – viewed from point of purchase rather than chart position. They embody a music industry that was still emerging from its subservience to light entertainment to become the prime generator of youth culture.

Many music outlets were located within department stores or music and/or electrical shops – like the examples shown here from Allen's, Clarke's and Rumbelows. They spread right across the country: concentrated in London, Manchester and other big cities, of course, but present too in Northampton, Scarborough, Chesterfield, Tunbridge Wells, Leicester and Loughborough. This was not the economy of a London elite but a teenage culture that – attracted by the efficiently targeted youth media of the day – was truly nationwide.

Spanning mostly from the 1950s to the 1980s, many of the designs here are immediately evocative: the rather dubious 1970s swirl of Virgin Records (see pages 218–221), the inspired 1950s moderne of C.R. Spouge (see page 46), the lines and circles that reproduce the contours of 7-inch and 12-inch vinyl. One of my favourites is the totally blank white bag of Cheapo Cheapo (see page 50), the notorious storefront and basement in Rupert Street, Soho, that was so cheap and contrary that they couldn't be bothered to commission and print a design.

Also present and correct are the specialist shops catering to hardcore mods, Rasta and other music/ fanatical subcultures: John Abbey's Contempo Soul Source or the bad-tempered Daddy Kool to name but two. Until the late 1960s, many black American records were available only imported by mail order or from specialist outlets and the same thing happened in the 1970s with the increasing popularity of reggae and dub. You had to be in the know.

What I find rather disturbing is how many of these bags are from shops I visited, if not haunted, back in the day. They read like a secret diary of my adolescence and young adulthood: Dobells, Harlequin, Harrods, HMV, Honest Jon's, Musicland, One Stop, Record and Tape Exchange, Rough Trade, Soho Records and Virgin Records. Dobells and Honest Jon's were particularly popular because they sold old records in a period when once a record was deleted, that was it. That's where I found the first two 13th Floor Elevators albums.

There are two outlets with which I have a more personal connection. My paternal grandmother was of the Crane family (see page 58): this was, as Trunk describes it, 'a global supplier of instruments, with at least ten huge stores in the North of England. The famous Liverpool store incorporated the existing Epstein Theatre, alongside workshops and offices. Records were only a small part of the company business, which finally closed in the mid-1980s.' To celebrate this, I found a Cranes' 78 bag – the only one of these artefacts I own.

Squire of Ealing, my early-1960s local, was on the Broadway near Haven Green. It was, as Trunk writes, a 'musical instrument and electrical repair shop'. Passing through the rather stodgy ground floor – full of wood: pianos and radiograms – you'd find a circular staircase that took you to the basement. Here was the record bar, decorated, as I remember, in a futuristic style that blended perfectly with the strange, eldritch sound of contemporary hits such as 'Telstar' and 'Hey Little Girl'. A pre-fame Dusty Springfield worked here.

Pop was the future then, a beacon taking us early post-war children out of austerity, deference and parochialism. Like Squire, many record shops constructed an environment – or at least a close-connected experience, as you pushed your way to the counter – that emphasised an extreme modernity and sense of community. This book reclaims many lost outlets – lost to the vagaries of time, taste, technology and urban planning – to construct a consumer-led social history of a still powerful and inspiring moment.

· · · Your Local Record Shop · · ·

SOUTH HARROW ——	305, Northolt Rd., South Harrow. 01 — 422 0122
NEASDEN ——	258 Neasden Lane, Neasden, N.W.10. 01 — 450 7802
RUISLIP MANOR ——	120, Victoria Rd., Ruislip Manor. 01 — 713 3653

Ref. No. 3757

INTRODUCTION

JONNY TRUNK

It must have been the late 1970s when I tentatively started visiting record shops. There were a few in my local towns of Aldershot and Farnham – Ken's Records, Elephant, Venus, Boots, Woolies, Spinnerdisc. Each varied in size, stock and atmosphere: some were welcoming, even exciting, while others could be seriously intimidating. And grumpy. Possibly a bit on the grubby side too.

By the early 1980s, Venus in Farnham had installed a Space Invaders machine. It stood next to the rack of rock posters (an integral part of record shops at that time) and on Saturdays drew a lively and even slightly criminal element. Because of the crowd gathered around the machine, we were able to spin a 10p piece into the 50p slot without being noticed and get three games for less than the price of one.

The biggest vinyl emporium was Boots in Farnham, which occupied the whole of the chemist's sizeable first floor and carried massive displays advertising new album releases along its walls. These were constructed from dozens of empty sleeves stapled into elaborate patterns and snaking shapes, often with added life-size cardboard cut-outs of artists or giant logos (such as Roger Dean's YES, carved from polystyrene). These items all had stickers on the back bearing the names of local fans who wanted to take the promotional material home when the displays were dismantled a couple of weeks later.

I didn't purchase many records in those very early days of my record-buying life – I hadn't yet discovered the sound that grabbed me enough – but I do remember that every shop produced its own bags in which buyers would carry home their spoils. The Boots 7-inch and 12-inch plastic bags were distinctive and colourful, appearing to focus on bluesy hairy rock. The Woolies plastic bag always seemed to be red and white but was different every time, featuring the Winfield logo somewhere or everywhere. And if you bought from WH Smith, the bags were always paper.

As my interest in records grew, so did my shopping territory, often expanding to the nearby city of Guildford where I would visit the punky and slightly scary Subway (always with a row of wildly dressed, angry-looking teens pressed against the large clear windows). It was here in 1981 that I bought my first Echo And The Bunnymen record ('A Promise'), a purchase made entirely on the strength of the band's name as I knew nothing about their music. When in Guildford I would also drop by the more laid-back (and slightly musty-smelling) Collectors Records Centre. This was where (circa 1983) I first came across Ian Clarke, who would sell you super-rare American jazz, soul and Latin LPs from his special 'jazz box' on the floor behind the counter – the type of dance records played at hip London jazz clubs by DJs such as Paul Murphy.

By the mid-1980s, the Our Price records chain was expanding, as was HMV, and on special occasions (like a Friday night) I'd drive to Piccadilly Circus in London to do a spot of late-night shopping at the all-new mega and multi-floored Tower Records emporium, a shop with a big department for every genre. It was super impressive, with cool, knowledgeable staff, extraordinary cut-out polystyrene displays for new artists and albums, and thousands of imported records and obscure cassettes from all over the world (I first bought 'Head' by The Monkees on tape there). The shop even hosted personal appearances: in 1988 I had my 'Lovesexy' LP signed by Prince and the band members. All very exciting.

As a scaled-down advertisement, bags played an important role in record-shop branding as well as in positioning collectors within a hierarchy. They became a symbol of record-buying seriousness:

your bag made a statement about you. So I'd prance around with freshly bought LPs in my 58 Dean Street bag, assuming that anyone who recognised it might deduce that I was into spy jazz, Mancini and loads of other film-music composers they'd never heard of. Or, even better, they'd not even heard of the shop and would wonder what on earth I'd been buying. There was also the joy of walking into a record shop carrying another shop's bag, prompting the counter staff to ask what you'd just bought (or I'd just tell them anyway, because a lot of record buyers – especially me – are desperate to tell anyone about their purchases). You can't see through most plastic or paper bags, so the contents would be a mystery. And if those contents were revealed, it might well be a 'got that' or 'desperately need that' or even an 'oh my god, you bought that!' moment. You could easily go out record-shopping

on a Saturday (immediately after payday) and bump into people with multiple bags all bursting with wax. (I was also buying heavily from charity shops at this time, but they never gave you a bag for a 10p LP.)

By the early 1990s, I found myself in the thick of it: living in London and buying every weekday from new and secondhand specialist shops in the West End, hitting markets and record shops in the suburbs at weekends or travelling further afield with fellow collectors on day trips to any reachable town or city. At the time there were no robust record-carrying shoulder bags, so a good, strong LP-sized plastic bag from a record shop would last several months as the 'carry all'. With lots of LPs being traded or swapped along with the bags they came in, the following three decades were a blur of bags and vinyl.

More recently – certainly over the last fifteen years – more record sales have taken place online, and of course there are no bags at all, just cardboard mailers. Over that time I've also seen a lot of record shops disappearing. There was a large secondhand classical shop in Norwich that I loved visiting: I would spend hours there, digging through badly organised boxes of classical records in the hope of finding a misplaced jazz or experimental LP along the way. That went about a decade ago. There were several grubby shops in Brighton (like Fat Geoff's Musicland – three floors of music and a fishtank) but these all seemed to disappear as the road near the station became a little less hippie and a little more gentrified. Naturally, loads of shops in London have gone, especially around Soho, Kings Cross and Notting Hill, where vast rent increases have made trading records no longer financially viable.

I truly miss Stand Out / 101 – two shops in one, owned by Bill and Bill, who'd fallen out and stopped speaking to each other – and Mole Jazz, with its regular rare-jazz auction list and an owner who hated jazz and was really into country and western. There was the overpriced On The Beat (where you could barely understand the drug-addled owner) and Caruso & Company, with an infamous 'Last Rights' rack full of hilarious LPs – weird field recordings or international singers whom the owner reckoned sounded like 'bush turkeys'. There was the late-night Cheapo Cheapo, where the proprietor would insult any friendly tourist who walked in ('the only Beatles in here are crawling about on the floor'), and then of course Harold Moores, a large classical shop over two floors that was very shouty and impressive, with seemingly endless racks of catalogued composers, walls of opera and boxes of lowly scores, shows and exotica on the carpeted floor. I enquired there once (when I could get a word in between incoming phone calls) about religious records and Harold said he had a warehouse where there might be some. We met up later at the address (I took Martin Green and Jarvis Cocker along for the dig) and entered an extraordinary converted church on the South Bank that was packed full of LPs waiting to be sorted for the shop. Harold Moores closed in 2017, a victim of huge rent increases and vinyl-shopping lethargy. A skip of LPs was dumped

outside the shop. where a fierce vinyl feeding frenzy took place that made it into the pages of the *Evening Standard*.

As my record-buying has slowed over the last couple of years (a combination of insane price rises and dwindling space at home), I started to look back. I have many fond and vivid memories of shops that have now closed, of dealers who no longer deal, of rare discoveries in buildings that have since been demolished. I find myself trying to recall record emporiums that may not even have existed, or shops I know existed but whose names have escaped me – like the tiny one between Hammersmith and Chiswick that had a lot of rock 'n' roll but not enough room to turn around inside, or the one that opened on Hanway Street in 1993 (behind the Virgin Megastore), carrying a lot of Gainsbourg, but disappeared after about three weeks never to be seen again.

I started to think about tracking down old record shop bags. Initially I found the obvious Our Price and Woolies ones – distinctive, even slightly kitsch. Once I had a few, I decided to make some T-shirts, essentially because they were the sort of thing I wanted to wear – I mean, what says 'I've been shopping in record shops for decades' better than an Our Price tee?

I had a few T-shirts screen printed (none of your rubbish digital T-shirt printing in my world) and they looked fabulous and funny. The reaction was favourable and they sold quickly, so I started looking for more bags with a view to making more tees. One of my better finds was a bag from Ecstacy For Records, a Chelmsford shop that existed briefly in the mid-1970s. I loved the hand-drawn 1960s-influenced psychedelic artwork – picture a naked piper in an Art Nouveau-style circular glass paperweight. According to legend, it was a hip shop that was integral to the live music / pub rock scene as well as playing a part in the doomed Chelmsford 'City Rock' punk festival of 1977. After further research, I discovered that this was where Grayson Perry bought his first record – 'This Is The Modern World' by The Jam – so I visited his studio to give him a tee. We had a lovely chat about the shop,

"ECSTASY" FOR RECORDS

62, NEW LONDON ROAD, CHELMSFORD, Essex.
PHONE: Chelmsford 63369
Proprietor: Martin Havelin

which he remembered as having listening booths. He was also in the audience at the failed punk concert, which he described as the most punk thing he'd ever seen, with the unpaid scaffolders taking down the stage and lobbing bits of scaffolding into the crowd while Eddie and the Hot Rods played on. All these stories came out of just one little paper bag. I sold all the T-shirts and naturally I wanted more bags, so I decided to advertise:

Wanted: old record shop bags – paper and plastic. Cash waiting.

I had a mixed response, with quite a lot of calls along the lines of: 'I used to have loads of great old bags but I threw them all away a few years ago / a few months ago / last week.' And quite a few saying: 'I have Rough Trade East, Fopp, Flashback in Islington, Reckless, Sounds Of The Universe and the new RSD 2021 one if you're interested.' I passed on these contemporary bags as they are a little too new for my 'old' record shop bag collection.

Sometimes I'd get one or two great bags from a record collector having a clear-out; other times I'd luck out and get maybe ten or so from someone who was just pleased to be rid of them. My collection was slowly growing. I made more T-shirts. Musicwise was a popular bag-to-tee logo, featuring a little owl gesturing with one wing, with the word 'Musicwise' above it: irresistible.

Hermons Records was next, a bag from a defunct early-1970s record shop that had a good line in Northern soul, located in Preston's brilliant brutalist bus station. The church-like rendering of the bus station gave the subsequent T-shirt a strangely religious feel. This was followed by Save Records (see page 175) – a brilliant paper bag from a small chain of four shops sited in market halls (Bury, Radcliffe, Rochdale and Lincoln), established in the late 1960s by Simon Jones, the ex-Rochdale Football Club goalkeeper. Sadly, the Save Records shops have now closed, but they still operate a small online business under a different name. I contacted them and asked if I could make some tees and soon another great old record shop bag turned into another great T-shirt. I was well and truly hooked.

Before long, I was buying more old record bags than old records. I even bought a record on eBay and told the seller he could keep the vinyl as I just wanted the bag it was in. Every time I made a new T-shirt, I'd get brilliant emails from people who vividly remembered the shops, the owners, the records purchased, the shops next door, all sorts. Or I'd get slightly irate emails if I'd sold out of a certain size. Usually XXL.

I eventually got a call about my bag advert from a man called Leon who runs the British Record Shop Archive. This is an online labour-of-love resource for British record shop history: it is by no means complete and quite possibly never will be, but it's a welcoming place where people can share memories of lovely shopkeepers, record-buying tales, pictures and aspects of British musical history. We met a week later and I was totally blown away by Leon's collection – not just the sheer quantity, but also the styles, printing techniques, graphics and terrible drawings. It was like *The Music Library* book all over again, where free rein had been given to people who quite possibly shouldn't have been making artwork, with unexpected and sometimes brilliant results. Leon suggested we do some swaps as he had some doubles and I suggested we pooled our resources and made a book instead. He was up for the book.

On my weekly trip to Spitalfields market, I had a chat with clothing and music dealer John from Vintage Hackney Wick. He's always first to notice me wearing my record bag T-shirts and had been badgering me for months to turn the whole bag thing into a book. My reply had always been that I didn't have enough bags, but this time I told him about the bags I'd got from Leon and explained that the book was now on. Of course, John knew Leon and within the week John turned up on my doorstep with his brilliant collection of old record bags. Some of his extraordinary finds – such as Peckings and R. & B. were added into the mix.

Finally, I went to see my old chum Ben, proprietor of Ben's Collectors Records in Guildford, a small shop that has managed to ride out successive recessions, the rise of the internet, even a pandemic.

HERMONS
RECORDS

**FROM THE NEW BUS STATION
PRESTON
TEL. 56581**

Ben has been behind the counter of record shops for as long as I've been in front. Over time he has amassed a large collection of bags simply because he loves anything to do with records. He also gave me an old bag full of bags for the book.

Despite being packed with bags, this publication is by no means a complete account of every old record shop and we apologise (a tiny bit) if your fave shop from the past is not here. You can blame me, Leon, Fuel, Jon, Ben, other contributors, or the fact that the bag design was deemed too bad or too bland or that an example of the bag no longer exists. Also please remember that many shops – like Cheapo Cheapo – were so 'cheapo' they used unbranded plain bags.

It's worth pointing out that a number of the bags bear interesting signs of their journey: sometimes the names of tracks or records have been scribbled on them, or perhaps their former contents, or even the name of the original purchase. On one example, the words to a song have been written on the back (Celia's, see page 49). You might find the name of the shopper who ordered and paid for the record, which would then have been bagged up ready to collect (Harrisons, see page 88). There are also generic bags with a blank space for an individual shop name to be printed (see pages 7, 9 and 15). Of course, there are many examples of the classic candy-stripe bag and various versions of stripes and swirly-patterned blanks that could be printed up with your shop name and number if you were on a tight budget. James Hunt of Fulham, Lonsdale of Bristol and a company called Personality Bags seem to be the primary suppliers of these.

I'm not one for getting academic about the content of my books, but what I've realised with this project is that collecting all these bags together makes for something historically fascinating. This is the history of British high streets – and more likely side streets too. It's a history of entrepreneurs, of good and bad design, of Jewish people selling ska in a shop before anyone else in the UK (see R. & B. Record Shop, page 153), of long-forgotten mint-condition vinyl stashes being found (see Tipple, page 210), of the shop where Dusty Springfield worked (see Squire, page 188) and of the occasional unpleasant boss (see Rayners, page 157). It's also a history of changing shopping habits, changing fashions and changing your needle when the old one started to wear out.

It's quite sad to think that nearly all the shops featured here (hundreds of them) have disappeared. This could be through aggressive high-street competition, redevelopment, death of the proprietors or any number of other uncontrollable factors. I'm sure it's much the same story for most traditional high-street trades. But everything works in cycles: brand-new record shops are opening up – more than I can ever remember – to sell both old and new releases. Vinyl sales are up another 10 per cent in the UK this year, reaching their highest level for thirty years.

For some, LPs are now a lifestyle choice and vinyl (or 'vinyls' as some 'new buyers' call it) is even back in supermarkets. I've also heard that some 'new buyers' will purchase records as a tangible representation of their fave music: they have no intention of buying a record player, they just want a physical object (as well as the download and stream). Brand-new represses of classic LPs are bought because people don't want the crackle of a secondhand record and wealthy collectors want mega-rare releases in every genre so they can post them on Instagram. But whatever their reasons, it's still record-shopping, and if someone has actually gone to a record shop to make a purchase (or to click and collect) they will get it in a bag – and that's what this book is really about.

I've heard another record shop has just opened up around the corner, so I'm off to do some shopping. But I'm taking my own bag with me.

Classics
folk
SHOWS
Top Twenty
opera
albums
jazz
ballet
Big Bands
ROCK
SOUL
Instrumental
Symphonies
old time
Brass Bands
Waltzes
Country
CHORAL
CHAMBER
Concertos

0 3720 6

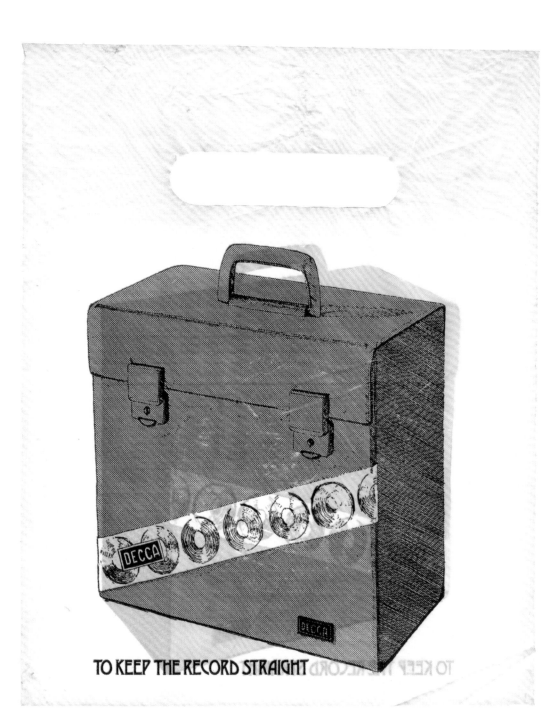

TO KEEP THE RECORD STRAIGHT

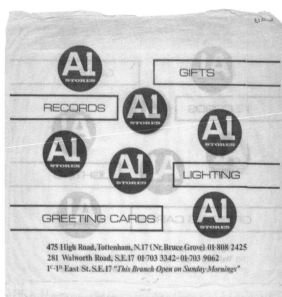

58 DEAN STREET

Springing from a branch of Harlequin Records in the late 1970s, this specialist shop quickly became the place to go for movie music and show LPs. Run by the Mascheter twins and their camp cohort Graham, it was a fount of knowledge for all things OST (Original SoundTrack). The shop was frequented by film fans and TV stars alike, with Danny La Rue often to be found holding court in double denim. It moved to Gower Street when rents in Soho grew too prohibitive, becoming Rare Disks, which closed in the mid noughties. And by the way – it's not 58 Dean Street, they all called it 'Five Eight Dean Street'.

A1

Established in 1912 and closed in 2008, this legendary family-run chain tempted many a pop star of the 1960s and 1970s into signings, appearances and launches. Sorely missed.

A. COOPER & SONS

An early gramophone retailer and and a shellac / vinyl dealer from the 1920s until the late 1950s. On the back of this bag is written 'Bill Hayley, Paper Boy / See You later Alligator', which dates it to 1956.

ADVANCE

A Leicester shop opened by Pete Jenney ('Leicester's very own John Peel') in the early 1960s. This op art bag, designed by Brian Plews, appeared in 1969. It was the first shop in the area to sell sell secondhand vinyl and to import rarities from the US. It handled gig tickets too – I mean, what else do you need? Closed down in 2006.

AERCO

Established in the 1950s, this record and specialist hi-fi retailer was named after the owner's son (Arnold E. Ricketts) and was taken over by family friend Mike Hall after Arnold died of leukemia. The shop moved into recording and label production, releasing a handful of records in the late 1970s. Eventually closed in the 1990s.

AJAX RECORD CENTRES

A small chain of Kent-based shops dating from the late 1960s. I have discovered very little information on them, apart from the fact that the owner drove an Aston Martin.

ALAN FEARNLEY

Opened in 1963 and closed in 2004, with just over forty years spent selling some great records and keeping up with changing tastes and sounds. The shop now sells online via MusicStack.

ALAN FREEMAN'S RECORD CENTRES

A chain of four stores in the London area capitalising on the celebrity of the top pop picker himself. Their life span was fairly short, as Alan 'Fluff' Freeman never set foot in one. Do we miss them? Not 'arf.

ALLEN'S

A radio services shop with a small but successful line in vinyl, early 1960s.

ALLEYCATS

Opened in the 1980s by 1960s rock 'n' roller Mick Robinson (who apparently wore a monk's habit on stage). More than likely specialised in super fun 'rock', rather than less fun 'pop'.

ALEX STRICKLAND

See Soho Records, page 182.

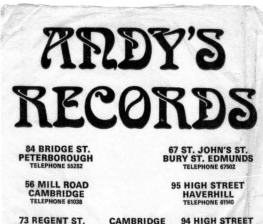

AL'S RECORDS

These popular North and East London record stores also ran a small line in sheet music. As far as I can determine, the shops closed in the mid-1960s.

ANDY'S RECORDS

Trading from 1969 to 2002, proprietor Andy Gray began with a small box of records on Felixstowe pier. By 1992 he had become the UK's largest independent music retailer. The rise of aggressive major high-street competitors slowly led to the chain's demise. Andy now runs BGO (derived from 'The Beat Goes On', his former shop in Cambridge), the successful reissue label.

ARCADE MUSIC SHOP

Established around 1960 by a Mr Rumbelow in North Finchley's art deco (but not so) Grand Arcade. The shop, complete with listening booths, was run with the help of his two sons. Eventually they focused solely on electrical appliances, but it had nothing to do with the other Rumbelows, if you know what I mean.

ARCADIA

My research uncovered confusing information about this being a 'new' old name for an 'old' old shop called Knights in Reading, established circa 1975 – which may well be the case. It is certainly nothing to do with the shamed high-street retailer Philip Green.

ART NASH

Opened in 1955 and closed in 2000. In its early days the shop specialised in jazz vinyl, then shifted to chart fodder in the 1960s, followed by a slow drift into musical-instrument sale and production. According to his grandson, Arthur Nash was 'a horrible git' who disinherited his children. See also Discassette.

ASTOR RECORD CENTRE

This lively Guildford shop with its many listening booths eventually became Derek's Records. Sadly now closed.

ATFurlong

music instruments records

AT FURLONG

This post-war record and instrument chain was established by A. T. Furlong and overseen by his son Vic (a big jazz and blues man), with branches in Bromley South, Bromley North, Deptford and Woolwich. It was in 1960, at the Bromley South shop on Saturday mornings and Wednesdays after school, that a fourteen-year-old David Jones first worked:

'It was here that the power of recorded music struck home. I don't mean it was where I discovered music, (I had already discovered that power through Little Richard and Elvis) no, it was more how those bits of black plastic could affect other people's behaviour.'
David Bowie, *A London Boy*

audiosonic

best records and tapes around....

12, Bell Walk, Eastgate Shopping Centre, Gloucester. Tel 0452 32280

Records, Tapes, Compact Discs, Bought & Sold

33 West Nicolson Street
031-668-2374

28 Lady Lawson Street
031-228-1939

AUDIOSONIC

Very little information can be found about this 1970s Gloucester shop situated in the newly developed shopping precinct.

AVALANCHE

This Scottish shop opened in 1983 – a perfect time to capitalise on the growing interest in Scottish independent music. And the great news is that Avalanche is still alive and kicking!

B-G RECORDS

We believe this was Brian Gilbert's shop in Stockport. We know little else, except that it was a lively punk hangout in the 1970s, with a small rehearsal room in the basement for local musicians. Brian also helped others to set up new record shops in the Cheshire area.

B-G RECORDS

16/18 LITTLE UNDERBANK
STOCKPORT
TEL:480-9441

backs records
3 swan lane
norwich

phone - (0603) 25658

BACKS

This important Norwich store, founded by Johnny Appel in 1979, was the epicentre of indie and punk in the 'fine city'. Running its own small label, the company became part of The Cartel distribution cooperative (see also Rough Trade and Red Rhino). After the shop's closure in 1991, ex-staff member Paul Mills went on to establish Soundclash records, which thankfully still survives.

BAKER'S

This record and appliance shop concentrated more on vinyl as it expanded into two further shops through the mid-1970s to the mid-1980s. It appears that Grays Records were also part of the chain, but details are unclear.

BARKERS'

Founded in 1913 and originally selling only pianos, by 1947 the shop catered in 'everything musical'. The record store ran until 1984.

BARNARD'S

This well-respected shop in Tunbridge Wells was established by the lovely John Barnard. His mother, who lived with him above the shop, would count the takings at the end of each day. Closed in the late 1970s.

BARTON & GINGELL

Opened in Battersea in 1957. From 1961, some mail-order adverts from this shop appear in editions of the *NME*, apart from this, little is known.

BAYES RECORDIUM

Opening above Bayes Television store in 1957, the shop moved to its own premises, complete with first-floor recording studio, in 1963. In 1973, the shop moved once more, this time to Kings Street, prompting a new bag design employing the 'Goodies / Spangles' font. The business was sold in 1997. A fondly remembered and influential King's Lynn hangout.

BEATTIES

This 19th-century department store had a small record section in the 1970s (possibly only in the Birmingham branch).

BENSTED'S

The shop was established around 1900, selling early gramophones and discs. If you wanted a snapshot of 1960s record shopping, it's perfectly illustrated on this bag: the shop is full of ladies, has a large counter with hundreds of records on the shelves behind, and three listening booths (although they could be the loos).

BERKELEY (Greenford)

Dating from the 1960s, now closed – no other information found.

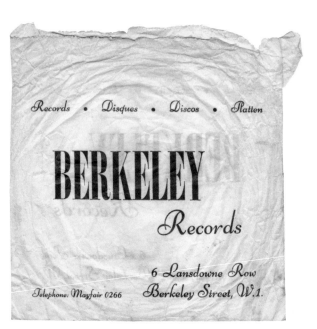

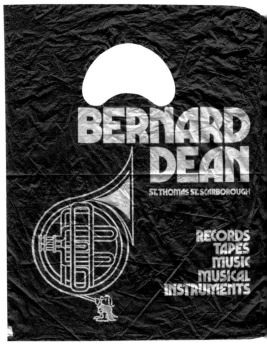

BERKELEY (Mayfair)

This shop was well posh. For a start it was in Mayfair, and just look at the bag with the word 'record' written in four different languages. Sophisticated or what?

BERNARD DEAN

This well-loved Scarborough record and musical-instrument retailer closed for business in the noughties.

BERNARD'S RECORD SHOP

Established by Bernard Klein, one of several family members who went on to open record shops. His brother-in-law was Paul from Paul For Music (see page 145) and close relations Derek (Derek's Records, page 62) and Nat Fox (yes, you guessed it, Nat's Records, page 132) followed suit. All were busy London shops, often with more than one outlet and market stalls thrown in for good measure.

BERWICK'S

The only thing we can tell you about this shop is that all the staff wore overalls and all looked like lab technicians, which is really brilliant.

BIBA

Founded in 1964 as a small mail-order company, by 1973 this iconic brand had opened a seven-storey flagship shop in Kensington, named Big Biba. The store's various departments were unified by a spectacular art deco-meets-surrealist interior design. The record department was home to an 8-foot diameter turntable, lined with record bins. The huge premises proved difficult to run and debts quickly mounted. A rescue package was put together to save it from closure, but Big Biba was forced to shut down in 1975.

BIRKHEADS

This old-school, small department store sold high-end electronics and hot wax. The store would close to the general public during shopping visits by celebrities who lived locally, including Tom Jones and The Beatles.

BERNARD'S
RECORD SHOP
2 IMPERIAL PARADE, NEW BRIDGE ST.
[10 YARDS FROM LUDGATE CIRCUS]   E.C.4
Telephone : 01-236 9915

Long Playing

Records

from

BERWICK'S
2 Sheep Street, RUGBY
TEL. 3337

BIBA

Walton's Leading Store

Radio Television
Records and Electrical
Goods

Birkheads
W. E. BIRKHEAD & SON LTD.

Cycles Prams
Toys Leather and
Sports Goods

CHURCH STREET
WALTON-ON-THAMES

Established 1750   Telephone : WALTON 20582/3/4

BIRMINGHAM CO-OPERATIVE SOCIETY
CO·OPERATIVE
SOCIETY
RECORD
DEPARTMENT
FOR ALL MAKES OF RECORDS

BIRMINGHAM CO-OPERATIVE SOCIETY

Their first store opened in 1881. Over a long period of expansion and after surviving two world wars, their first modern-day superstore was opened in 1971.

BLUEBIRD

A classic small chain of shops for soul, reggae, cut-outs, new imports, jazz-funk etc., and a true mecca for DJs and fans of such genres. Alive in the 1970s, thriving in the 1980s, this bird had flown by the 1990s.

BONAPARTE

This small Surrey-based chain specialised in modern soul imports and all things punk and goth. They also produced a small run of post-punk singles from 1978 onwards.

BOOTS

The well-established and much-loved chemists moved into music retail around 1960 and by the mid-1970s were shifting masses of music. I have no idea why they stopped – the 'company history' section of the Boots website doesn't mention music at all. There is a small school of thought that believes the blues rocker on the bag is Rory Gallagher.

BORDERLINE

A popular Brighton shop that opened its doors in 1981, eventually closing in 2014 following the growth in online shopping and increased business rates.

BOSTOCK'S

The shop was established by Gerry and Paul Bostock (father and son) in the early 1970s. It specialised in cut-outs (heavily discounted records, usually marked with a cut notch or hole punched in the corner of the sleeve), American pressings, imports and super bargains (like twenty records for a pound). After becoming part of the Dynamite Records empire (which started a doomed label and lost money on heavy TV advertising), the shop closed in the early 1990s.

BRADLEYS

Opened by multi-instrumentalist John Bradley, this chain expanded quickly across the North of England, even starting up an eponymous music label (responsible for Roy Budd's 'Diamonds' as well as several weird Goodies records). The business was finally eaten up by Our Price in the 1980s.

BRENDONS

This small group of well-to-do television, electrical, piano and record stores was a sister chain to Squire of Ealing, which would explain the similarity in their later bags (an early bag is shown here and a Squire bag on page 188). They were called Brendons after Mrs Squire's maiden name. Staff from both chains were moved between the shops according to departmental demand.

BRISTOL WIRELESS

A well-respected pair of city centre stores with particularly knowledgeable staff. Opened in the 1950s and closed in the 1980s.

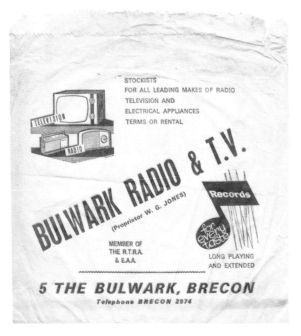

BRITISH HOME STORES

This large chain of department stores was founded in 1928 by American entrepreneurs. Some larger stores began to sell records in the 1960s, stopping in the mid-1970s. The 'Prova' logo on the bag was the BHS in-house label.

B.V. HICKS

Established in 1960, this Stowmarket business sold and repaired televisions and also dabbled in records for a short time, although white goods seemed a better and more profitable option. After fifty-four years of trading the shop closed following the rise in online commerce.

BULWARK RADIO & T.V.

This family-run business is still going strong but now sells only kitchen gear and electrical goods. Don't waste your time going there to look for any rare jazz or deadstock reggae – I've already been.

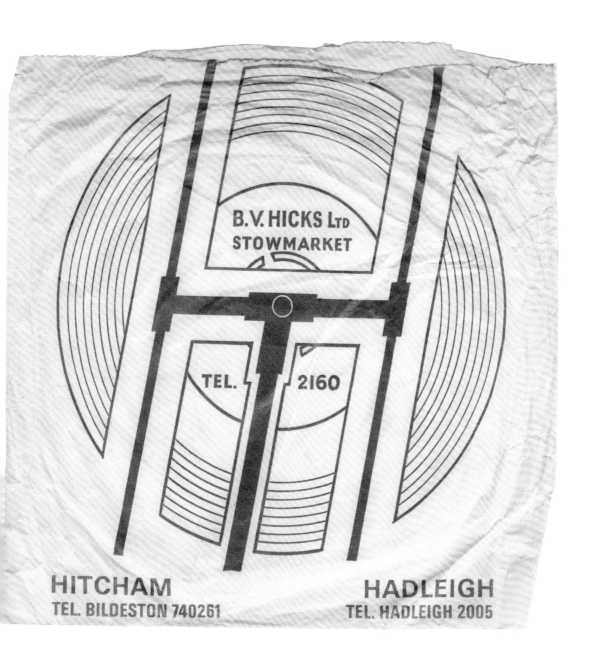

B.V. HICKS LTD
STOWMARKET

TEL. 2160

HITCHAM
TEL. BILDESTON 740261

HADLEIGH
TEL. HADLEIGH 2005

45

46

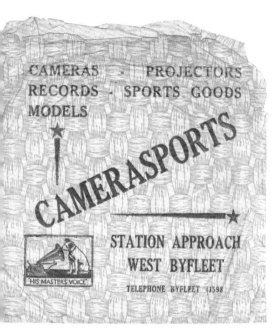

C.R. SPOUGE

A large electronics retail outlet with an impressive record shop at the rear which also offered efficient mail-order and import services. The shop closed in the 1970s after the owner died and the area was subsequently redeveloped.

CAMERASPORTS

A shop that sold models, camera gear, projectors, sporting goods and records (also opening another shop called Towerelectrics, again with no space between the two words). A heavenly mix of goods all under one roof – until they closed in the 1970s.

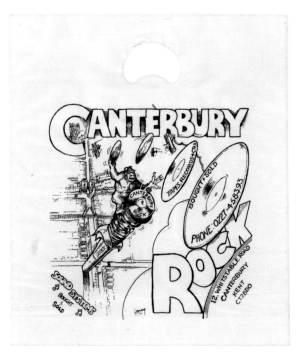

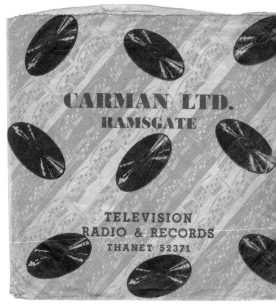

CANTERBURY ROCK

This Kent store was opened in 1979 by Jim Hampshire, the shop is still rockin'. According to one online review, 'the staff has a love of music'. Obviously. See also Rock Bottom page 166.

CARMAN

Purveyor of electronics and vinyl through the 1950s and 1960s.

CH RECORDS & TAPES

This one is a total mystery but the brown and gold say 1970s. Could CH stand for Challenger & Hicks?

CELIA'S

A chain of 1970s shops with a penchant for denim, heavy metal and big-selling pop. The lyrics to 'So You Win Again' by Hot Chocolate (1977) are written on the back of this bag.

CHALLENGER & HICKS

There were three branches of this record and music store, owned and run by Paul Jennings. He was the son of Tom Jennings, the inventor and producer of Vox guitar amplifiers.

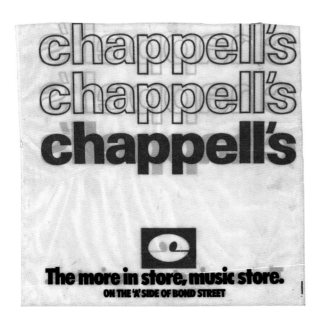

CHAPPELL'S

This large music publishing house opened a suitably large music store in Central London. The shop still exists in Wardour Street, but now only sells sheet music and instruments.

CHEAPO CHEAPO

The legendary late-night, multi-storey deletions shop in Rupert Street, Soho, complete with notoriously grumpy owner. It was rumoured that the deadstock LPs originated from the hijacked vans of major labels and vinyl factories. They were far too tight to have any bags printed.

CHEW & OSBORNE

This impressive Essex shop had a pretty nice carpet and some cool shelving too. Opened in the 1960s, it closed in 2013, long after it had stopped selling vinyl to concentrate on 'high fidelity equipment'.

CHRIS'S

Established in the late 1950s by W.C. and C. Casley as a fine specialist record shop with a lot of wild jazz. Still operating in the 1960s, but I can't be sure it lived out the decade. I blame the jazz.

CITICENTA

This 1980s London shop also took over the Readings For Records shop (see page 157) when the owner retired in 1983. The business went into administration in 1991.

CLARKE'S

Selling all things audio (they even had a transistor-radio repair service), this shop opened in 1960 and closed in 1982. The old and attractive double-fronted premises of the Wisbech branch is now a gambling den.

Chew & Osborne Ltd.

**148 HIGH STREET
EPPING, ESSEX
EPPING - 4242**

HIGH FIDELITY EQUIPMENT
TAPE RECORDERS
RECORDS

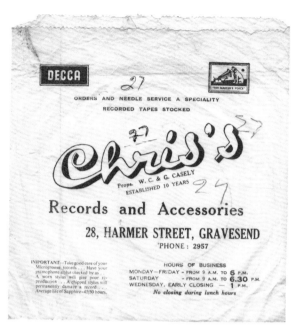

DECCA

ORDERS AND NEEDLE SERVICE A SPECIALITY
RECORDED TAPES STOCKED

Chris's

Props. W.C. & G. CASELY
ESTABLISHED 10 YEARS

Records and Accessories

28, HARMER STREET, GRAVESEND
'PHONE : 2957

IMPORTANT—Take good care of your
Microgroove records . . . Have your
gramophone records stylus checked by us . . .
A worn stylus will give poor reproduction . . . A chipped stylus will
permanently damage a record . . .
Average life of Sapphire—45/50 hours.

HOURS OF BUSINESS
MONDAY—FRIDAY - FROM 9 A.M. TO **6** P.M.
SATURDAY - FROM 9 A.M. TO **6.30** P.M.
WEDNESDAY, EARLY CLOSING — **1** P.M.
No closing during lunch hours

Citicenta Records, 43 St. Johns Road, London SW 11 1QW. Tel: 01-228 01

CITICENTA RECORDS

CLARKE'S

MUSIC   SERVICES

WISBECH
AND
SPALDING

CLIMAX FOR RECORDS

AND RECORD TOKENS

ACCREDITED DEALER

"HIS MASTER'S VOICE"

143 DUDLEY ROAD, BIRMINGHAM 18

Telephone: EDGBASTON 2440

CLIMAX

A music and electrical parts retailer from the post-war period, good for spares and the odd slab of brittle vinyl. The building was demolished in the 1960s as part of the Heath Street clearance scheme.

CLOUD 7

This small chain of shops had multiple outlets across London, including Portobello Road, Wimbledon and Hounslow (having bought out Musicland). They closed in the 1980s.

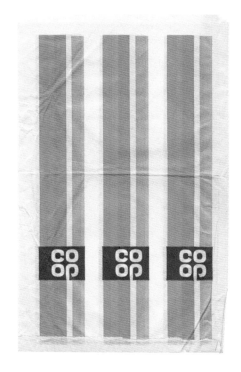

THE COOPERATIVE (CO-OP)

A consumer cooperative with roots going back to 1844, which set up a number of diverse retail businesses, including (from the late 1950s) well-advertised record departments in their larger stores. It's unlikely this foray into music lasted any longer than the early 1970s, but you could get Green Shield stamps with every single and LP purchase.

RECORD TOKEN BAGS

Record tokens were a common gift in my youth, particularly from aunties or uncles who were not up to date with my current listening habits. The tokens would always come in a printed greetings card, which was placed in the shop bag. Still available until the mid-1990s, they were mainly printed and issued by EMI and always watermarked to prevent forgery. Apparently record tokens were reintroduced in 2018, but I've still to come across their latest incarnation.

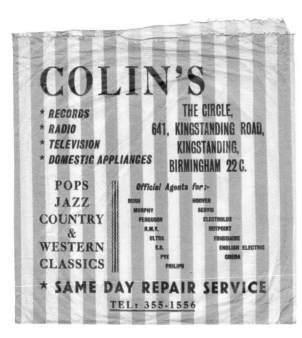

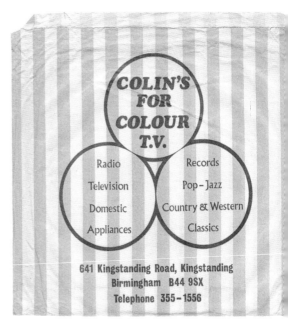

COLIN'S

This 1960s electrical and vinyl shop is not currently listed in the Birmingham Music Archive of record shops. It may well have been too terrible, or just better at selling televisions.

COLLET'S

The chain's fine bookstores in and around Central London also retained extensive and important record departments specialising in folk, jazz, world and field recordings. Bill Leader (recording engineer and record producer) worked in their folk department, while Shirley Collins (the famed folk singer) worked in the Haverstock Hill branch. When the New Oxford Street store was redeveloped a young employee named Ray Smith took over the dissolved jazz department and started Ray's Jazz Shop. In 1989 the Charing Cross branch was firebombed as part of the campaign against the publication and sale of Salman Rushdie's *The Satanic Verses*.

CONTEMPO SOUL SOURCE

This London record shop, mail-order service and label was established in 1970 by John Abbey, owner of *Blues & Soul* magazine. Rather than your usual 'shop', it was more of a first-floor room, located above a wine bar. It imported, sold and issued some absolutely killer soul. One of the most important and influential record shops of the 1970s, the operation closed in 1979 when Abbey married and moved to the US.

CRANES

A music-shop empire that had its beginnings in a pawn-broking business established by the Crane family in 1876. After moving into the importation and manufacture of pianos and organs, by 1910 the company was a global supplier of instruments, with at least ten huge stores in the North of England. The famous Liverpool store incorporated the existing Epstein Theatre, alongside workshops and offices. Records were only a small part of the company business, which finally closed in the mid-1980s.

CURTIS

Starting as a small chain of electrical retailers in the 1920s, by the 1950s W H Curtis boasted record bars (cool hangouts – a bit like an alcohol bar with records, but serving only coffee) and a 78rpm cutting studio. A larger record store was opened in Sheffield town centre, followed by others across Doncaster and Nottinghamshire. By 1973 the entire chain of stores had closed down.

DADDY KOOL
RECORDS

94 DEAN STREET
LONDON W.1
TELE. 01-437 3535

THE REGGAE
SPECIALISTS

DALES

Agents for
GRUNDIG Tape Recorders

"HIS MASTER'S VOICE"

Harmonicas, Radiograms, Records & all Musical Goods

Music Stores
High St., TENBY

Telephone 2285

DANCY'S
for
★ R:E:C:O:R:D:S ★

21, Silver Street, EDMONTON, N.18
7, The Broadway, EDMONTON, N.9

'Phone : EDM 4724

RECORDS

DANCY'S
46 SOUTH MALL · EDMONTON · N.9
PHONE 807 4724

DAVIDS RECORD SHOPS
1 Chalton Street
Euston N.W.1.
Tel. No. 01-387 8651

20 Covered Market
Slough   Bucks
Tel. No. SL 24310

2 Market Place
Bracknell Berks
Tel. No. Bracknell 22395

DELMAR'S MUSIC SHOP LTD

Stockists of all Leading Records

107 DARKES LANE
POTTERS BAR
HERTS.
Tel : PR 56723

DEREK'S RECORDS are at
6 TURNPIKE LANE N.8. 340/3438
9 WENTWORTH ST. E.1. 247/1797
107 FORE ST. EDMONTON N.18. 803/1090
11 THE ARCADE, WALTHAMSTOW E.17 521/1955

DEREK'S

RECORD & TAPE

CENTRES

3-5 WENTWORTH STREET E.1.
247/1797

DEREK'S

11 THE ARCADE, WALTHAMSTOW
E.17.
521/1955

RECORDS

1 NORTH MALL, EDMONTON GREEN
SHOPPING CENTRE N.9.
803/5506

DEREK'S CUT THE COST OF LISTENING

DADDY KOOL

Established in the early 1970s, these shops could be found at various Soho locations, above and below ground, until their closure in 2003. A killer and often quite intimidating reggae specialist, it's where I bought my copy of 'Greedy G' by the Brentford All Stars in 1992, having tried to sing it to the dreadlocked man behind the counter, who immediately identified what I was going on about.

DALES

A family-run, music-based business set up seven decades ago, still going strong, and still run by the Dales. At 89, Laurie Dale (son of the original owner) is the oldest music retailer in the country. On Sundays he plays his favourite easy listening in the shop.

DANCY'S

This shop first opened 'for records' in the 1930s. Two of their stores were still trading in the 1970s, but little information can be found after that.

DAVIDS

A small chain of London shops and stalls operating from 1961 onwards. The owners were Neil and Roy Joseph, not David, as you might have assumed.

DELMAR'S MUSIC SHOP

A very small shop opened by a bloke called Eric Delmar in 1964. Unconfirmed reports state that his brother-in-law had opened the Arcade record shop in Finchley a few years earlier. Delmar's is now closed down.

DEREK'S RECORDS

This chain of London shops owned by Derek Fox and Terry Harrington operated from the early 1960s to the late 1980s. Apparently all the records played by WIllie Morgan, who DJed before kick-off at Tottenham Hotspur's White Hart Lane ground, were always from Derek's Records, and he'd let the crowd know that over the tannoy at every game.

DIAMOND

Operating from 1965 to 1981, this shop specialised in soul and reggae, consequently attracting a bit of a mod scene at weekends.

DISC EMPIRE

Opened by Tony Monson in 1978. He had previously worked as a pirate radio DJ and started the UK's first mobile disco business. This shop at World's End stocked (and supplied wholesale) jazz-funk and soul imports from America and Japan alongside much more. The shop closed in 1981 and Monson has since done a lot of work with Solar Radio. What I'd give to see the old stock from his Empire now!

DISC RECORDS

This shop opened in the 1950s and finally closed in the mid-1980s. Refusing to move with the times, they still had 78s on display the week they shut down. The free gift / winning number idea on the bag is pretty exciting though.

DISC-N-TAPE

A cool shop on the legendary Gloucester Road where there were loads of second-hand shops selling everything you want but don't actually need. The shop closed in 2006.

DISC JOCKEY

Established in the 1960s, the shop was bought by Alan Jensen when the original owner, Johnny Hodgeson, became a local councillor. The 'DJ', as it was affectionately called, was located in the 'old town' part of Hastings. With a knack for advertising, Jensen was known for his interesting (and slightly controversial) promotions and sales ideas. The shop was sold to Our Price in 1984.

POPULAR
JAZZ
CLASSICAL
RECORD SPECIALISTS

DIAMOND RECORDS

(CATFORD)

199 RUSHEY GREEN
CATFORD, S.E.6
01-698-9739

DISC EMPIRE

402 KINGS ROAD
CHELSEA, LONDON S.W.10
TEL: 351 1433
352 6861

★ RADIO
★ RECORDS
★ REPAIRS
★ TELEVISION
★ Record Players
★ Terms Available
★ Tape Recorders
★ Electrical
Accessories

FREE GIFT

THIS WEEK'S WINNING
NUMBER ANNOUNCED
NEXT SATURDAY

13 551

DISC RECORDS

(MORDEN) Ltd.

HEAD OFFICE :
40 ABERCONWAY RD.
MORDEN

DISC-N-TAPE

17 GLOUCESTER ROAD

BISHOPSTON

BRISTOL BS7 8AA

TEL: 422227

DISC JOCKEY
FOR
RECORDS

TELEPHONE
2031

2 QUEEN'S ROAD
HASTINGS

THE DISC JOCKEY

2 QUEENS ROAD • HASTINGS • Tel.: 422031

RECORDS, CASSETTES & CARTRIDGES

DISCASSETTE

If you ever see a posh choir singing, all the choristers will be holding a well-crafted leather folder, containing the words and music. These folders were originally made at Art Nash (see page 27), but the building was sold in 1971 and the business moved to a shop in Weybridge that also sold records ('disc') and tapes ('cassette'). It seems that the main part of the Discassette business was making these superb choir folders. The company still flourishes today under the same name, but stopped selling vinyl decades ago.

DISCI RECORDS

This chain was established by Barry Class, record dealer, hustler, landlord and manager of multi-racial pop darlings The Foundations. He ran the short-lived Trend label from the Westbourne Grove head office and shop. At the peak of business in the mid-1960s, he had eleven shops, with the late-night Piccadilly Circus stores witnessing regular queues. All are now gone: it's possible fraudulent activity could have been at the bottom (or top) of it.

DISCLAND

This well-positioned store, close to the local college, sold lots of jukebox singles to teens back in the 1950s, 1960s and 1970s. Both the college and Discland are no more, but I think the world 'browserie' may live again soon in some small gentrified enclave. Also, remember the guy on the bag – the little Bellboy character. He'll be popping up a few more times...

DISCO TWO + 2

All we know about this emporium for soul, pop, reggae and imports is that it was established by Bert Rand.

DISCOS

A short-lived chain of two stores from the 1960s–1970s. They sold Peter and Gordon records, of that we can be certain.

DISCOTRAK

Little is known about this shop, which opened in 1975. Apparently, it sold good contemporary music, eventually closing and reopening as What Records in the same town.

DOBELLS

Legendary – and we mean legendary – jazz shop, born from Doug Dobell's father's antiquarian bookshop at 77 Charing Cross Road. From a small stash of imported jazz 78s, the music shop grew into a full-on jazz hangout, issuing jazz, blues and world music on its own 77 label from 1957. In 1963, Bob Dylan (as Blind Boy Grunt) played in the shop basement. Another blues-based, mail-order shop was opened in Rathbone Place, which subsequently shut down, the stock moving back to Charing Cross. Dobell died in 1987, and the shop finally closed in 1992. I visited around 1990 and it was full of cigarette smoke, fairly empty wooden racks, and sadness.

DOBELL'S JAZZ RECORD SHOP

77 Charing Cross Road, London, WC2 GERrard 4197
Dobell's Folk Record Shop.
75 Charing Cross Road, London, WC2 GERrard 5746
Home and overseas Mail Order Service

DOWN BEAT

This classic basement shop in Lower Marsh, Waterloo, could only be accessed through the ground-floor vintage-clothing emporium, via a perilous staircase. Once down there, a constantly spinning 1950s Thorens turntable would be used to audition original Jamaican 7-inch singles, which were instantly sold to the collectors and DJs lined up at the tiny counter. A memorable and knowledgeable store. Opened in the 1990s, it closed in the noughties.

DOWNTOWN RECORDS

With its roots as a market stall in 1960s Basildon, run by the Spellman brothers, the first shop was opened by local celebrity Noel Edmonds, who brought the area to a standstill. It developed into a successful and influential chain, apparently a hotbed of punk and Oi! with some fascinating and rowdy happenings in-store, including a member of staff being taped to a chair and placed on top of the counter (allegedly).

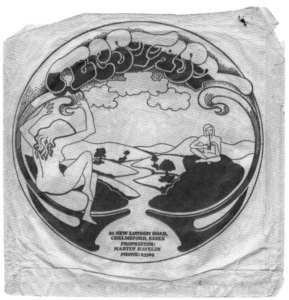

DUB VENDOR

This retailer of rebel music began life in 1976 as a market stall in Clapham Junction, opening its first shop in Peckham in 1977 and a Clapham branch in 1982. Remaining founder John MacGillivray expanded the business to incorporate mail order (and later established the legendary Record Shack in Ladbroke Grove). Over the next three decades this was THE place for dub in the capital. The growth of online business meant that by 2011 the retail stores had closed. The company now operates online only.

ECSTASY FOR RECORDS

Established in the early 1970s by Martin Havelin, this shop – complete with listening booths – briefly became the focal point for both recorded and live music in Chelmsford. Havelin was a main sponsor of the disastrous *City Rock* punk festival, which took place on 17 September 1977 at Chelmsford Football Club stadium. I'm not sure if this led directly to the shop's closure, but it certainly didn't help to keep it open.

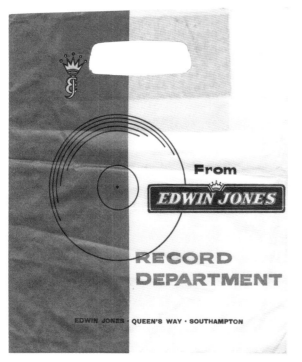

EDWIN P. LEES / PICCADILLY RECORDS

In 1978, this chain of white-goods retailers opened a record department in their Manchester branch. Located in the Piccadilly Plaza, the shop became known as Piccadilly Records. In 1983, when the Edwin P. Lees chain closed down, the newly redundant record shop staff took out a loan and reopened Piccadilly Records in nearby Brown Street. The hugely respected and very busy store has won numerous awards including *Music Week*'s 'Best Independent Music Store'. The dancing figures on the bag are taken from Letraset sheet AA125, as previously seen on The Human League's 'Being Boiled' single artwork.

EDWIN JONES

This Southampton-based department store opened in 1860 and was purchased by Debenhams in 1928, but continued to trade under its own name. After the original store was destroyed in the Blitz, it was rebuilt in 1959 in a brutalist style. In 1973 the company was finally renamed Debenhams.

Edwin P. Lees
(RECORD DEPARTMENTS)

67 NEWPORT STREET,
BOLTON
Tel: 32121

48 ABINGDON STREET,
BLACKPOOL
Tel: 20147

- RECORDS
- TAPES
- VIDEO TAPES
- COMPACT DISCS

Edwin P. Lees RECORD DEPARTMENTS

**MARSHALL'S RECORD CENTRE
& PICCADILLY RECORDS**
PICCADILLY PLAZA   PICCADILLY GARDENS
MANCHESTER.   Tel: 061 236 6501

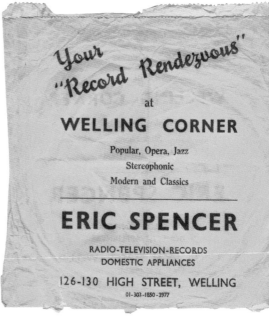

ELECTRICAL SERVICE

Apart from the bag being practically illegible, we can tell you that these two shops date from way before 1966, because this is when all-figure dialling was introduced and the old area mnemonic (here BAY as in Bayswater) was dropped.

ERIC SPENCER

The idea of a 'Record Rendezvous' suggests to me that this business wanted groups of young people to come to the shop to 'hang out'. Still open in the 1970s, we have no information after that date.

EVANS

Another shop established by Bert Rand, selling soul, pop, reggae and imports (see Disco Two + 2, page 66).

F.H. ALCOCK

Purveyors of 'the finest novello melodies' from the 1950s onwards – but not that far onwards, as they closed down in 1969.

F.J. GRAHAM

This short-lived specialist in Herne Hill served the local community with blues, R&B and Elvis throughout the 1960s.

F.J. LOCK

This shop was opened in 1948.

Records
from:-

EVANS

YOUR **KING STREET** RECORD SHOP
TEL. **MAIDENHEAD** 1820/1

RE-CONDITIONED
UPRIGHT and GRAND
PIANOS
BY ALL THE BEST MAKERS

F. H. ALCOCK LTD.
for
THE LATEST RECORDS

RADIO
AND
TELEVISION

LONDON HOUSE,
61 HIGH STREET,
E V E S H A M.

PHONE : 2288.

RECORDS
TAPES
ACCESSORIES

F. J. GRAHAM

**RECORD
SPECIALISTS**

232 RAILTON RD., HERNE HILL, S.E.24
TEL. 01-274 7046   (Opposite S.R. Station)

BLACKFEN PRINTING SERVICES / SIDCUP

F. J. Lock

ALSO
ELECTRICAL RETAILER

**GRAMOPHONE
RECORDS**

87, STATION RD, TAUNTON, Som
TELEPHONE 2988

FARMERS

This once thriving business lasted for a century, opening in 1880 and closing in 1980. More details on the shop (and forty-nine other lost Luton stores) can be found in Bob Norman's book *Were You Being Served?*.

FARRINGDON RECORDS

A small chain of stores in Central London, specialising in classical music. This bag dates from the 1980s.

FELDMAN'S OF SOHO

During the 1960s this music publisher (very) briefly dabbled in selling records. These might well be the only two bags they ever gave out.

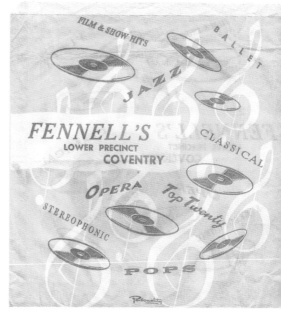

FENNELL'S

This long-standing Coventry record emporium has made it into the list of 'Coventry shops we miss', along with Blockbuster, Woolies and the pick 'n' mix section at Happy Shopper.

FENTON SMART

For some, everything you need in life is represented by this bag. Opened in 1972 by David Fenton, this cool mod emporium stocked clobber as well as vinyl. Things went well until the chain stores moved into Putney in the 1980s. Now closed down.

FINLAYS

In the poptastic mid-1960s, this Whitehaven sweet shop decided to open a record 'department' out the back. Then they closed it.

FOLLETT'S AND WYNESS

These popular South London shops supplied chart hits alongside guitars and even gave a bit of help with tuning. They seem to have thrived in the 1960s, but had all disappeared by the end of the 1970s.

FRANCIS RECORDS

This was a bit of a spooky, multi-doored, two-floored shop, run by the Francis family. During the mid-1960s, the mother, aged over sixty, was in charge of the rock and pop section. The shop survived until 1985. It's the sort of grotty hole I would have stumbled across in the backstreets of Southampton in the early 1980s.

MENSWEAR

BOYSWEAR

RECORDS

CASSETTES

FENTON SMART

2 Medfield St., Roehampton, S.W.15   Tel. 788-7695

RECORD DEPT. 1968

All Sizes and Speeds
Available.

Finlays

Records Specially Ordered
on Request

9,
Duke Street,   WHITEHAVEN
CUMBERLAND

YOUR RECORD CENTRES
FOLLETT'S AND WYNESS

RECORD
TOKENS

GUITARS,
Etc.

L. T. BAWCUTT

5 LORDSHIP LANE, DULWICH, S.E.22 — 01-693 1450
455 HIGH ROAD   183 HIGH STREET
LEYTON, E.10   DEPTFORD, S.E.8
01-539 2406   01-692 1887

FRANCIS
RECORDS
LTD.

POUND TREE ROAD
SOUTHAMPTON
Telephone 21417

SHEET MUSIC RECORDS
FRANCIS DAY & HUNTER
INSTRUMENTS ACCESSORIES

138-140, CHARING CROSS ROAD, W.C.2. PHONE 01-836-9351.

FRANCIS DAY & HUNTER

This long-established, Soho-based music publisher opened a shop at their Charing Cross Road headquarters, selling sheet music, instruments and a very large selection of vinyl. In fact, through the 1960s they had possibly one of the largest record departments in London. Just like every other Soho music publisher, they eventually realised there's more money and a lot less hassle in publishing music rather than selling records.

FRED H. FEY

In my search for information on Fred H. Fey, all I could unearth was a series of really rare UK soul records (like The Marvelettes' EP), all with Fred H. Fey stamped on the reverse. He was certainly open in the 1950s, but it's doubtful he was still around by the late 1960s.

GILBERTS

This longstanding record shop was opened in the 1950s and still had two busy listening booths in the 1970s.

GILES

A pair of 1970s record shops in Redhill and Reigate.

GOOSES

Starting out as Goose And Sons, this chain of four record shops was spread out across the UK. They opened a second Norwich branch in 1966 (at the ceremony, the ribbon was cut by daytime TV and housewives' favourite, The Bachelors), which closed two years later. In the 1970s, the Croydon store was said to be the best-stocked record shop after HMV on Oxford Street. The shops had apparently all closed by 1978.

GRANT ELECTRICS

No prizes for guessing that records were not the primary source of income for this particular Birmingham consumer electronics store.

GRIFFIN BROTHERS

The Griffin brothers – Ron, Jack and Bert (three of seven children) – were electrical geeks. Their father, a farmer and beekeeper, had been killed by his bees (while I know that's not relevant, it is quite interesting). Anyway, the brothers were not into bees, but they loved electronics. So in 1928, they opened an electronics shop. By 1931, things were thriving and they moved to larger premises. In 1961, they decided to enter the record-selling market. This was rather short-lived, as we believe they stopped selling records in 1962. The electrical shop closed in 1983, with the last remaining brother passing away three years later.

GROOVE RECORDS

A 1980s Soho haven for soul, electro, jazz, US imports, hip hop and early house. It closed in the early 1990s, possibly following fierce rent increases in the area. The label Citybeat was run out of the shop, and a fledgling XL Records started as an offshoot in the late 1980s.

GUILDFORD RADIO

I like the fact that this place had a record salon. I think this could well be the future. I can see a very expensive record salon establishment, stocked with pricey vinyl, like a Discogs wants list, but with a front door and a sofa.

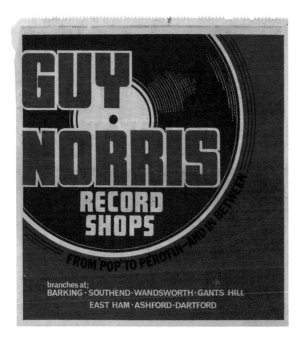

GUY NORRIS RECORD SHOPS

FROM POP TO PÉROTIN—AND IN BETWEEN

branches at;
BARKING · SOUTHEND · WANDSWORTH · GANTS HILL
EAST HAM · ASHFORD · DARTFORD

THE BEST IN RECORDS and TAPES

GUY NORRIS

POPS · JAZZ · CLASSICAL

barking
594-5245
gants hill
550-0637

wandsworth 870-1017
and branches

east ham
552-2082
southend
610631

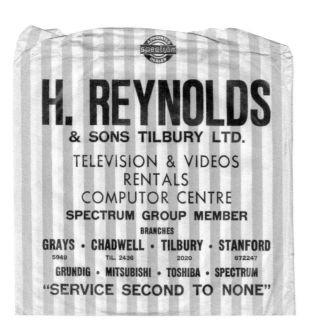

H. REYNOLDS

& SONS TILBURY LTD.

TELEVISION & VIDEOS
RENTALS
COMPUTOR CENTRE

SPECTRUM GROUP MEMBER

BRANCHES

GRAYS · CHADWELL · TILBURY · STANFORD
5949   TIL. 2436   2020   672247

GRUNDIG · MITSUBISHI · TOSHIBA · SPECTRUM

"SERVICE SECOND TO NONE"

15475

RECORDS   TAPE RECORDERS   TELEVISION

HAMPTONS of KENSINGTON

Donald Pears
&
Jimmy Young

WASHING MACHINES   RADIOS

harlequin record shops

HEAD OFFICE 67 GT. TITCHFIELD STREET, W.I TEL. 636 1348 BRANCHES THROUGHOUT LO[

sounds

MUSIC IS THE MESSAGE

harlequin
RECORD SHOPS

HARLEQUIN

TELEPHONE
01-907 8863

287 KENTON LANE,
KENTON, HARROW,
MIDDLESEX,
HA3 8RR.

RECORDS & TAPES

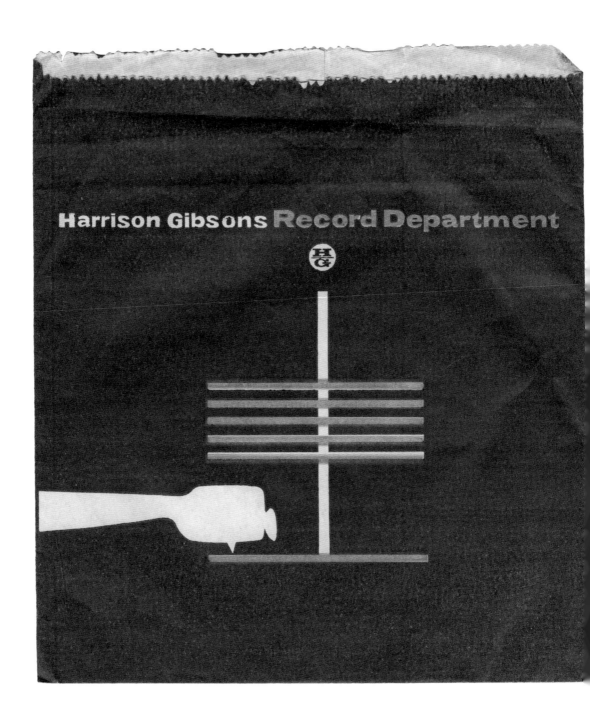

HARRY HAYES

847 Fulham Road SW6 736 4597

203 North End Road West Kensington W14
Tel: 385 1481

Stereo Tapes & Cartridges

records

MADE & PRINTED BY: HANCOCK COLLIS & CO. LTD, 315 KENNINGTON ROAD, LONDON, S.E.11, TEL: 01-735 1488

GUY NORRIS

This small chain of stores started in Barking in the 1960s and expanded throughout the 1970s. They were particularly punk-friendly when that scene took off. The shops also played video clips on in-store monitors, which was pretty cool back then. Incidentally, Billy Bragg's first job was working behind the counter in the Barking branch.

H. REYNOLDS

At first glance you'd think this bag was from the 1950s or 1960s. Well, it is actually a 1982 bag with the word 'computer' spelled wrongly.

HAMPTONS

A 1960s home-electronic retailer with a clichéd idea of what a record bag should look like.

HARLEQUIN

A great chain of 1960s record shops opened by former ice-cream vendor and entrepreneur Laurie Krieger. Harlequin, with its late-night, 24-hour attitude, expanded in the 1970s to a total of sixty-four shops, with specialist outlets for genres such as country music and blues. One of the branches features in the film *Confessions of a Pop Performer* (1975), involving a light sex scene with a member of the band 'Kipper'. By 1980, most of the branches had been sold to the rapidly expanding Our Price.

HARRISON GIBSONS

Yorkshireman George Harrison Gibson opened a tiny furniture shop in Ilford, Essex, in 1902. Most people thought he'd fail as the town was so small, but Ilford grew quickly and Gibson's shop with it. After burning down in 1924, the shop was rebuilt on a grander scale, only to be destroyed again by fire in 1959. The next incarnation of the building was a cool multi-storey modernist construction (designed by Forrest & Barber), complete with ribbon windows and relief cladding, which possibly influenced the bag design. Packed full of fine furniture to suit all tastes, it also had a record department on the upper floor. Unfortunately, this lasted less than a decade before being replaced by more furniture. Eventually other department store brands began selling their wares in the shop: the subsequent lowering in quality led to a drop in custom and the store was shut. The building has been empty for years and its future remains uncertain. Personally, I'd just turn it into one massive new record shop.

HARRISONS

Very little is known about this shop. Perhaps someone could call Gulliver 2900 for me and try to find out what the devil happened to this large place full of interesting and slightly worldly music.

HARRODS

Back in the good old days (the 1920s), Harrods was very different to how it is today. As well as a large and expensive gramophone department, it even had a dancehall. By the 1960s, it had a cool music department selling cool audio systems and even cooler records. It was still selling records into the 1980s. Perhaps it will start to sell new vinyl again if the prices keep rising.

HARRY HAYES

These popular West London record stores were established in 1950 by Harry Hayes, the son of a bookmaker and a reasonably successful trad jazz sax player. Hayes produced several records as a band leader for HMV, but retired from the jazz world in the mid-1960s to concentrate on retail. At one point he had three shops, but all were closed by the mid-1980s. Hayes died in 2002, aged ninety-two.

HARUM

This chain was established in 1975 by Graham Umbo and Mick Harding, hence the amalgamated shop name 'Harum' (personally, I think Harumbo or even Hardumbo would have been better). They expanded quickly to five shops, with one opposite Church Studios in Crouch End, which meant that the occasional pop superstar would drop by. The quick rise of the compact disc format saw the speedy fall of the Harum chain and by the mid-1980s, all the shops had closed.

Your Friendly Music Shop

POP - JAZZ - CLASSICAL
IRISH and GREEK RECORDS

Phone: Gulliver 2900

HARRISONS
MUSIC CENTRE

Large selection
of slightly used records

Why not come and browse through our
Long Playing Department at your leisure

Thousands of LPs. and EPs. to choose from

253, CAMDEN HIGH STREET. LONDON. N.W.1

GRAMOPHONE DEPT.

Harrods
KNIGHTSBRIDGE

HARRY HAYES RECORDS

Stereo Tapes & Cartridges

847 FULHAM ROAD, S.W.6   Tel. 736 4597

203 NORTH END RD. WEST KENSINGTON   Tel. 385 1481

HARUM
RECORDS AND TAPES

DISCOUNT SHOPS
CROUCH END OI-348 7038
MUSWELL HILL OI-883 6076
BARNET OI-441 3816
WATFORD 34013
WEST HAMPSTEAD OI-794 8000

HARVEY'S

From what I can gather, 1 Station Place seems to have been the site of many other record shops including Harvey's. However, the last time I checked it was an oriental take-away called Wok U Like.

HENRY'S

In 1956 Henry Sansom spent £400 opening his first shop in Southampton. In 1959 he moved to larger premises, eventually closing in 1988 thanks to aggressive chain-store competition.

HENSLER BROTHERS

This lovely paper bag has survived when little else about Hensler Brothers remains. They sure knew how to utilise punctuation!!

HERMLYN

A great bag from a pretty standard rock and pop store from the mid-1970s.

HIDES

From humble beginnings, this department store, established in 1851, eventually occupied a fine art deco building on Bexleyheath's Broadway. The store had its own deli, as well as selling furniture, china, clothing and, of course, stereos and records. It was forced to close in 1979, when the building was demolished to make way for the Broadway Shopping Centre, a bland brick box that looks a bit like a chicken farm.

HIGH HILL BOOKSHOP

Set up in 1956 by charismatic 'bookman' Ian Norrie, this shop was perfectly situated to cater to Hampstead's arty, bibliophile residents. It became one of the leading independent bookshops in the UK, and undoubtedly sold spoken-word and poetry-based LPs at the record counter. It closed down in 1988, in the face of mounting chain-store competition and the collapse of the public library market.

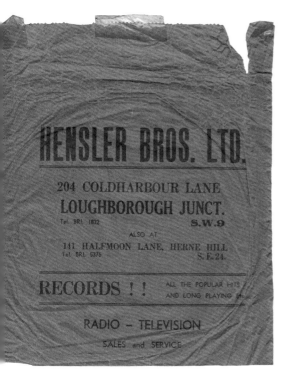

HENSLER BROS. LTD.

204 COLDHARBOUR LANE
LOUGHBOROUGH JUNCT.
Tel. BRI. 1832   **S.W.9**

ALSO AT

141 HALFMOON LANE, HERNE HILL
Tel. BRI. 6376   S.E. 24.

RECORDS !!   ALL THE POPULAR HITS
AND LONG PLAYING 33

RADIO — TELEVISION
SALES and SERVICE

hear it at hermlyn

hermlyn

hermlyn

eltham high street se9
the catford centre se6

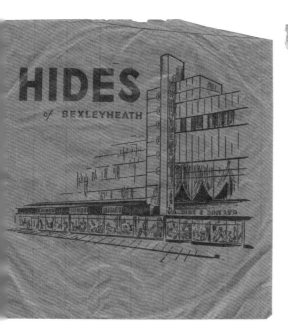

HIDES
of BEXLEYHEATH

HIGH HILL
BOOK SHOP

RECORDS - BOOKS - CARDS
ARTISTS MATERIALS

11-12 HIGH STREET, HAMPSTEAD
Telephone : HAMPSTEAD 2218   N.W.3

HMV

The first HMV-branded store opened in Oxford Street in 1921. After being damaged by fire in 1937, it was reopened in 1939 with Sir Thomas Beecham cutting the ribbon. In the mid-1960s, the business started to expand across the UK, becoming the largest retailer of music, with more than three hundred stores by the mid-1990s. Around 2013, the empire began to crumble, with administration, takeovers and all sorts of other big-business badness. It is important to mention that in the 1960s the Oxford Street flagship store was a record-buying heaven, complete with listening booths, an export lounge, hi-fi department, weird wire shelves for records, state-of-the-art furniture, a personal record 'salon' and more. Bring it all back, I say!

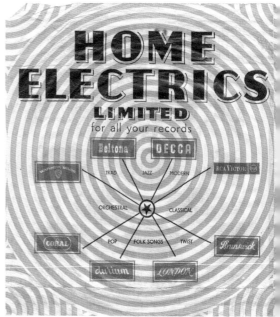

HOME ELECTRICS

A great set of shops where you could buy a fridge and some cool tunes simultaneously.

HONEST JON'S

This internationally known jazz and reggae hangout was started by Jon Clare in Golborne Road, moving to Portobello Road in 1982. In the 1980s and early 1990s, the basement was crammed full of killer secondhand US and Euro jazz, with a cool mini reggae shop behind the counter on the ground floor. It's still there and still jumping, thanks to Mark Ainley and Alan Scholefield. However, the basement is now used for record storage and a slightly odd loo.

HOUSE OF ANDREWS

This ancient and important Durham bookshop (with links to Conan Doyle) was taken over in 1963 by four talented young men and expanded to sell sheet music, records, stationery and paperbacks, A small restaurant was added in 1964, as were 'listening cubicles'. By 1980, it was no longer profitable and was turned into a newsagent.

HOWARD'S DRUG STORE

This has to be one of the best shops in the book – simply because of the name. Drugs and records: they go together, if you ask me. It was located in the underpass at Old Street tube station back in the 1970s, when the area was a lot rougher and nowhere near as fashionable as it is now.

HUDSONS

This fabulous musical store and vinyl shop opened in 1905 to serve the people of Chesterfield. It closed down in 2012.

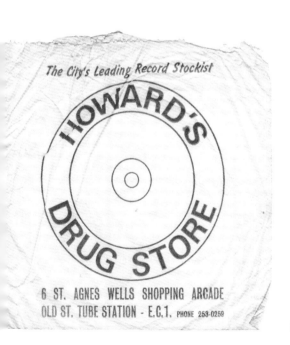

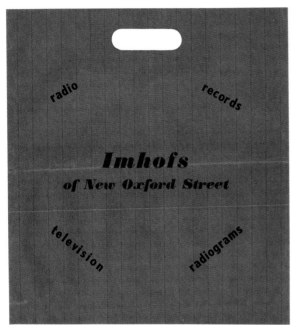

IMHOFS

Established in 1845 by Daniel Imhof to sell musical instruments as well as his one-off musical inventions. The shop became the first to sell gramophones (in 1896) as well as His Master's Voice recordings (from 1901) and early bamboo and cactus gramophone needles. By the 1960s, Imhof's in New Oxford Street was a four-storey emporium importing rare American albums, with a classical music department, a melody basement for pop, listening booths and a hi-fi equipment floor. It's now a Starbucks, with none of the above.

IT – INTERNATIONAL TIMES

The groovy counterculture / anarchist newspaper was launched by John Hopkins and Barry Miles in 1966. This bag may well have come from the Uncommon Market, an event held at The Roundhouse in January 1967, when lots of people got together to sell records and books and clobber and futiques (yes, futiques – FUTure anTIQUES) among other things. And all to raise funds for IT. But the bag does say IT Records & Tapes Ltd, and as hard as I've searched, I can find absolutely nothing about this failed IT venture. Perhaps it never even happened? It's exciting to know that potential information is out there waiting to be discovered and I will continue in my quest to find it. I've even contacted Barry Miles himself: at this point all, I can say for certain is that (1) Barry hasn't got back to me and (2) the bag is super rare.

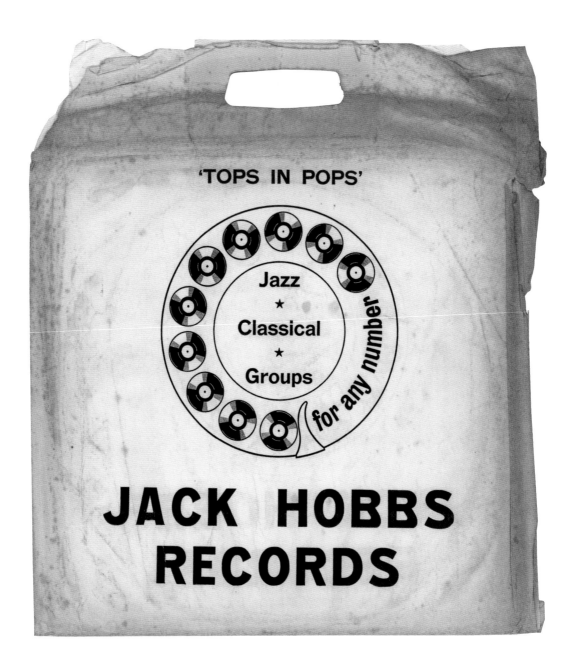

'TOPS IN POPS'

Jazz
★
Classical
★
Groups

for any number

JACK HOBBS RECORDS

JACK HOBBS

A small Eastleigh-based shop selling discount LPs, Music
For Pleasure box sets and ex-jukebox fare, alongside radios.
It closed down in the mid-1980s.

JILL HANSON'S

Established by Jill in 1957, and at that time the only record shop in Coventry. She'd received a good grounding in the retail business after working at her grandfather's piano and sheet-music shop. The 'Record Shop Queen' remained until 1981, when rate increases finally forced closure.

JOE'S RECORD CENTRE

Established in 1967 by Trinidad-born Joe 'the boss' Mansano. With direct business links to the fledgling Trojan label, the shop was an instant success. Joe moved into reggae production and was given his own Trojan subsidiary label called 'Joe'. By 1976 reggae styles had moved on, and Mansano closed his shop and returned to Trinidad.

JOHN JAMES

A chain of Bristol electronic and radio shops set up by philanthropic ex-RAF man, John James. At its peak there were more than 300 stores. James also set up a foundation for education and health that is still active today.

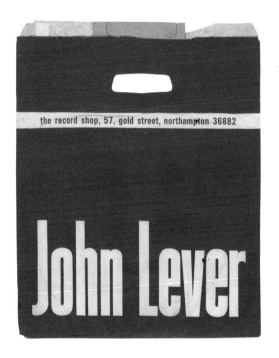

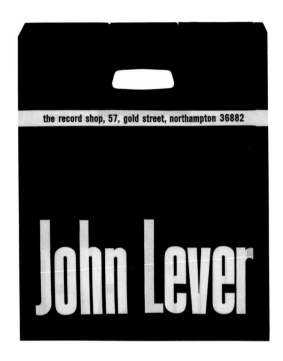

JOHN LEVER

Opening in 1954, on Kettering Road, this was the first specialist outlet of its kind in Northampton. In 1959, a larger shop, devoted solely to records, was opened on Gold Street. This specialised in jazz and American imports, possibly to cater for customers from the nearby US air base. Lever died aged fifty-four, but his family carried on the business, which finally closed its doors in 1985. Great bags, with regular colour changes. The orange bag we feature here was given to a customer who bought a copy of 'Led Zep II' at the shop.

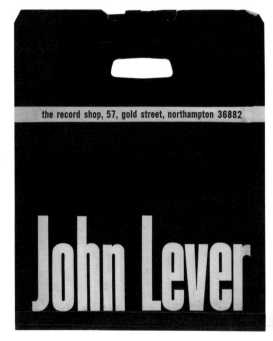

the record shop, 57, gold street, northampton 36882

John Lever

JOHN MENZIES

Founded in Edinburgh in 1833, this was the first bookshop to stock Dickens' published work. The firm expanded into a large chain of railway-platform bookshops. By 1968, they had 350 railway bookstalls and more than 160 shops. It's likely that the bigger stores began to sniff around the record business in the 1970s, but they had abandoned any ambitions in this area by the late 1980s. I'm not sure about the 'another record from John Menzies' tagline, as I never bought the first one.

JOHN OLIVER

This shop opened in 1965, opposite the big Woolworth in Redruth. It closed in 2007, and for a while was taken over by Oliver's daughter and her husband (also called John). But their shop sold cards and was called The Emporium. This has also since closed.

JUMBO

Founded in 1971 by Hunter Smith, the shop took its name from its owner's mobile disco: Jumbo Disco Services. It first opened in the Queens Arcade, Leeds, then moved to the Merrion Centre in 1974, where it stayed for the next two decades. When Smith retired, the shop was taken over by two dedicated customers and it is currently back in the Merrion Centre following a stint at the St John's Centre (from 1988). It represents an important part of the Leeds music scene and the logo is still exactly the same. Cool.

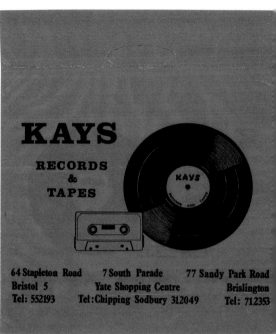

KAYS

RECORDS
&
TAPES

64 Stapleton Road   7 South Parade   77 Sandy Park Road
Bristol 5   Yate Shopping Centre   Brislington
Tel: 552193   Tel:Chipping Sodbury 312049   Tel: 712353

KAYS
Records & Tapes

7 SOUTH PARADE, YATE SHOPPING CENTRE.
TEL. C/SODBURY 312049
64 STAPLETON ROAD, BRISTOL BS5 0RB. TEL. 552193
77 SANDY PARK ROAD, BRISLINGTON. TEL. 712353

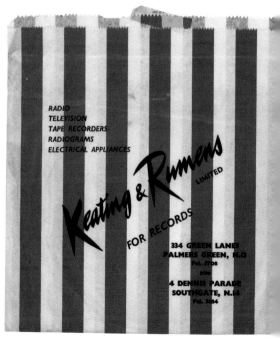

RADIO
TELEVISION
TAPE RECORDERS
RADIOGRAMS
ELECTRICAL APPLIANCES

Keating & Rumens LIMITED

FOR RECORDS

334 GREEN LANES
PALMERS GREEN, N.13
Tel. 3708
also
4 DENNIS PARADE
SOUTHGATE, N.14
Tel. 3684

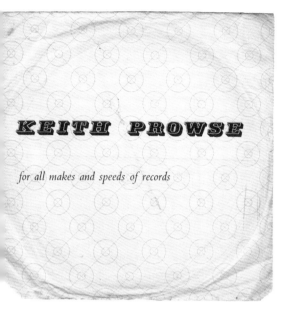

KEITH PROWSE

for all makes and speeds of records

KEITH'S RECORDS

KELLEYS RECORDS

Brentwood 2671   Southend 63991   Basildon 21636

Kelleys records

Brentwood 215519   Basildon 21638   Southend 63991   Chelmsford 66164   Romford
Braintree 25930   Highlands 78268   Hadleigh 556815h

KAYS

I found a 1972 photograph of Stapleton Road in Bristol and there was Kays (with a Cortina MK1 parked outside). Apparently, the neighbourhood was redeveloped and traffic rerouted, and the area fell into rapid decline. I believe the shops managed to hold on into the early noughties.

KEATING & RUMENS

This pair of short-lived record shops opened in the early 1960s and closed in the late 1970s. It is now a stationers.

KEITH PROWSE

This chain had eight shops in London with offices selling tickets for gigs and a 'budget plan' department, allowing you to buy records using a hire purchase-style system. And of course, a standard record-buying counter. The shops were bought in 1971 by the Ali family, an entrepreneurial bunch who bought up several chains (including Musicland) and had their own vinyl distribution company.

KEITH'S RECORDS

This shop was opened by Keith Southwell in 1966, in the town of March, Cambridgeshire. It was THE teen hangout for the area. Now it's a shop called Pornbroker's Gold, where less amazing memories will be made.

KELLEYS

A small Essex chain that started in 1960 as quality hi-fi stores with record departments on the first floor. Continued trading into the 1980s.

KENDALLS

Established in 1970. The business is still going strong as a large electrical-services group based in Telford.

KEN PALK

I can tell you that the proprietor of these two popular shops died aged eighty-two in 2010. I believe his stores were open throughout the 1970s and 1980s to service the busy areas of Bramhall and Knutsford but closed in the 1990s.

KEN'S RECORDS

This bag is from Aldershot, where I grew up. It pretty much sums up the town and the shop: a bit cheap and a bit grotty.

KENNY'S RECORDS

Apparently this oldies specialist is where Sheffield legend Richard Hawley bought his first record. It is now a Martins Good To Go food shop.

KETTS

Originally established as a bicycle repair shop in Isleworth in 1946, by 'Pop' Prickett. The shop also sold electrical goods, which outperformed the bicycle side of things – so much so, that their second shop in Kensington only sold electrical goods, expanding to twenty-four branches by 1959. In the 1960s and 1970s, records became a small extension to their sales of record players and hi-fi goods, but this was often nothing more than LPs and singles on carousels inside or outside the shop. By 1988, all branches of Ketts had closed.

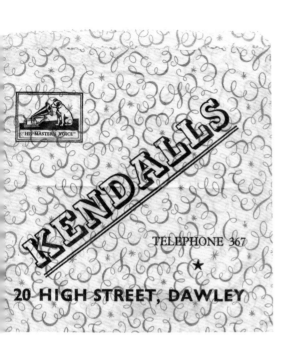

KENDALLS

"HIS MASTER'S VOICE"

TELEPHONE 367

20 HIGH STREET, DAWLEY

KEN PALK LTD. BRAMHALL 8479

KEN'S RECORDS

RECORDS AND TAPES BOUGHT
FOR CASH

Large stocks of both new & secondhand records

13-15 UPPER UNION STREET
ALDERSHOT, HANTS.
Tel: Aldershot 22155

Specialists In All Types Of Deleted Records

KENNY'S RECORDS

L.P. & C.D.   45 R.P.M.

32 THE WICKER
SHEFFIELD S3 8JD

From The 50's To Now

KING DISCS

This 1970s and 1980s destination for all things music also branched into the video rental world in the 1980s.

KINGSON'S

These popular South London stores sold a variety of instruments as well as vinyl and shellac formats. Established in the 1950s, they lasted into the 1980s.

KIOSK

I really like this. Not just a newsagent, but also a coffee house and record hangout – in fact, a 'phono-disc record bar'. We badly need to bring these back. I believe Kiosk is still open, but there has been no vinyl inside the shop for at least four decades.

KNIGHTS

This Caversham shop sold toys on the ground floor and vinyl downstairs. One local commented that this was 'the ITV to WH Smith's BBC'.

L. & H. CLOAKE

These 1950s London stores slowly expanded across South London and beyond. Then, just as slowly, they started closing branches until, around 1983, they had all disappeared.

LCS

This is a bag from The London Cooperative Society. Formed in 1920, this should not be confused with the Co-Op: it was a consumer cooperative society (owned by consumers and democratically managed). By 1952, it had more than 500 associated cooperative organisations, ranging from small shops to large retail outlets.

KIOSK (PONTEFRACT) LTD

NEWSAGENTS

HIGH CLASS
SWEETS
TOBACCO
CIGARETTES
GREETING
CARDS
TOYS, ETC.

ALSO IN CASTLEFORD, AIREDALE AND FEATHERSTONE

Phono-disc Record Bars
PONTEFRACT AND CASTLEFORD

MON-AMI Coffee House
PONTEFRACT

KNIGHTS

L & H. CLOAKE LTD
FOR ALL YOUR RECORDS

34/36 The Boulevard, CRAWLEY, Sussex
Phone: CRAWLEY 25135
131 London Road, EAST GRINSTEAD, Sussex
Phone: EAST GRINSTEAD 21866
262 High Road, STREATHAM, S.W.16. Phone: 769 7304
29 High Street, CROYDON. Phone: 686 1336
2 Central Parade, 5 London Road, REDHILL, Surrey
Phone: REDHILL 62798

22, Churchill Square, BRIGHTON Sussex Phone: BRIGHTON 202060

popular hits and makes in Stock

RECORDS
RECORDS
RECORDS

LCS

CASCADES CENTRE
FREDERICK STREET · ROTHERHAM
66606

THE RECORD STORE
WITH LOTS, LOTS MORE!

12 Station Road, Bishops Stortford
Tel 506621

LASER

This short-lived 1980s vinyl emporium opened in the all-new Cascades Centre, built around 1981. I had a look at the centre, and although the name suggests 'free flowing', the architecture conveys the opposite. It's likely that Laser were squeezed out a few years after opening, when the big chains moved in.

LAWES

Longstanding retailer for electrical goods, electrical repairs and vinyl sales, moving into video rentals. Closed in the noughties, and is now an estate agent.

LEADING LIGHTING STORES / LEADING RECORD STORES

'Open Sunday Mornings' as stated on the bag is most unusual as most stores back in the 1960s and 1970s were shut on Sundays. So an early seven-days-a-week shop.

LEAPFROG

A cute bag from a record shop that shut down in 2013.

LEATHER LANE MUSIC SHOP

A Central London store that traded from 1964 to 1976 and was managed by a man named Arthur. As part of the small Paul's Music record chain, the bags were printed on both sides with each shop name.

LESLIE BROWN

A late-1940s record shop established by ex-military man Leslie Brown, who also ran a 'personal recording service' in the studio below. The results were often labelled 'A Brownie Recording'. By the 1960s, he had expanded into toys and clothing. The shop closed down in 1991.

LEVY'S

Established in 1890 by the Levy family, the company initially sold sewing machines and hired out bicycles. Branching into the fledgling gramophone and music market, they began importing hot jazz, built their own recording studio and even started their own label. By the mid 1950s they'd won the contract to produce (and press) soundalike recordings of pop hits for the Woolworths Embassy label. So successful had the shop, studio and pressing business become, that it was purchased by CBS in 1964.

LEWIS'S

A chain of department stores started in 1865 and purchased by Selfridges in 1951. In the 1960s, the large shop in Birmingham had a very cool music basement with listening booths and more. Went into administration in 1991.

LEWKS

Established by Lawrence Welham and his business partner Keith Edwards in 1973, the shop name is an anagram of their initials (according to Lawrence, it could well have been KEWLS, WELKS or SKEWL). Trading for more than forty-five years from a small town a few miles south of Kings Lynn, Lewks became the biggest music retailer in Norfolk. The shop finally closed in 2018, when Lawrence hit seventy.

LION RECORDS

Came in just like a lion in 1978; went out like a lamb in 1984.

LLOYD & KEYWORTH

This shop was in my hometown. By the time I had got to record-buying age (the late 1970s) it was a 'don't touch that' type of electrical and camera shop, with a bit of a snooty attitude to youngsters. And there were no records anywhere.

LISTEN
98 HIGH STREET
BLACKWOOD
RECORDS & TAPES
TELEPHONE
WOODFIELD 362

more records from

MANN'S MUSIC SHOP

THE HOUSE
OF RECORD SERVICE
123 HIGH STREET

PHONE COLCHESTER 72783

LP LOW PRICE RECORDS

SPECIALISTS IN DELETED
❋ RECORDS & TAPES ❋
&
❋ OVER STOCKS ❋

BRANCHES THROUGHOUT
LONDON & ESSEX
HEAD OFFICE 01-555 4321

ANOTHER RECORD

FROM

"LULLABY OF BROADWAY"

8 CHIGNELL PLACE
WEST EALING, W.13

(CUL-DE-SAC, 10 YDS. FROM OLD HAT PUBLIC HOUSE)

PHONE: 567-1396

PROGRESSIVE, TAMLA
REGGAE, SOUL, POPULAR, Etc.

IRISH
COUNTY & WESTERN
DEPT. UPSTAIRS

BOOKS and RECORDS

M & J PARKES

4 STATION PARADE
NORTHOLT RD SOUTH HARROW
01-422 3548

IMPORTERS OF AMERICAN RECORDS

RECORDS ARE NOT EXCHANGED ONCE PURCHASED

Magills Irish Records & Books

107 GOLDHAWK ROAD · LONDON · W.12 · 01-743 7149

MARSDENS

RECORDS · HI - FI · RADIO · T.V. · ELECTRICAL

79-81. High Street Waltham Cross.

Telephone: Waltham Cross 22554

MARSHALL'S
RECORD CENTRE

RECORDS

223, WILMSLOW ROAD
RUSHOLME
MANCHESTER 14

Telephone RUS 7984

OPEN TILL EIGHT

MASCALL

RECORDS

2, OLD BROMPTON ROAD, SOUTH KENSINGTON, S.W.7

(CORNER OF HARRINGTON ROAD)

Telephone: KNightsbridge 4698

MAX
RECORDS

4 Grove Road, Eastbourne, E. Sussex. Tel: Eastbourne 36292

LISTEN

The only thing I could find out about this shop is that it was located in the small Welsh hometown of The Manic Street Preachers. No idea who the singer on the bag is.

LP / LOW PRICE

Throughout the 1980s this small chain was chock-full of deleted stock (unsold, unwanted, unfashionable stock from major labels that had been dropped from their current catalogues) and all sorts of other cheap, black treasure. Further branches were located in Barking and Manor Park.

LULLABY OF BROADWAY

This West Ealing shop was run by husband-and-wife team John and Olive, with a good reggae section plus Irish and country sections upstairs. It was a regular haunt of TV and film stars, because of its proximity to Ealing Studios. Dennis Waterman was often seen shopping here.

M & J PARKES

1970s South Harrow shop for books and imported records.

MAGILLS IRISH RECORDS

In 1974, there were two Magills stores, selling Irish records, books and tapes.

MANN'S MUSIC SHOP

Established in 1854 by Frederick Mann, this is one of the oldest music shops in the UK. It is currently run by Tim Mann, great-great-grandson of the founder. You can see what the shop looks like by the bag. Sadly they don't sell records any more.

MARSDENS

This is a poor excuse for a record shop really, as their main focus was on electricals. They were quickly relegated into second place in the vinyl stakes when Opus Records opened in the area.

MARSHALL'S

This 1960s and 1970s Manchester store had two outlets; today there are none.

MASCALL

Run by charismatic Londoner Harry Morgan, this shop was a favourite haunt of South Kensington celebrity residents such as Dana Gillespie. Great taste in blues and jazz.

MAX

Opened by Max Kenny, this small shop rapidly expanded to larger premises before being killed off when Our Price set up in town. Kenny moved into music promotion, founding the company 3MV in 1992.

MAXWELL

Established by E. H. Maxwell at the turn of the 20th century, supplying all things music to Woking, possibly even Paul Weller. Maxwell was a local businessman who formed the Woking Choral Society. The shop continued well into the 1960s, selling pop hits alongside instruments for up-and-coming beat-group combos.

MAYNE & SONS

Popular chart music and electrical retailer for a busy suburban enclave. Closed in the 1970s.

MEDHURSTS

Originally a drapery store opened by Fred Medhust in 1879, the shop grew into the largest department store in Bromley. By the 1950s, they had a thriving record and gramophone department, run by a gay couple named Jimmy and Charles. The author Paul Trynka states in his book *Starman* (2012), that a young David Bowie gained his musical education in this very store, using the listening booths after school on many occasions.

MAXWELL

for

Everything Musical

PIANOS • TELEVISION • RADIO

RECORDS

MAXWELLS OF WOKING (WOKING 4032)

★ Music, Pianos, Television, Radio, Hi-Fi ★

IN THE INTEREST OF CUSTOMERS, RECORDS CANNOT BE EXCHANGED

DECCA

LONG PLAYING 33⅓ RPM

UNBREAKABLE MICROGROOVE

RECORDS and REPRODUCERS

TELEPHONE YOUR ORDERS TO BEACONSFIELD 89

TELEVISION
•
RADIOGRAMS
•
RADIO
•
RECORDS
•
ELECTRICAL
HOUSEHOLD
APPLIANCES

Mayne & Sons of

BEACONSFIELD

SUPPLY

EVERYTHING FOR THE RECORD COLLECTOR

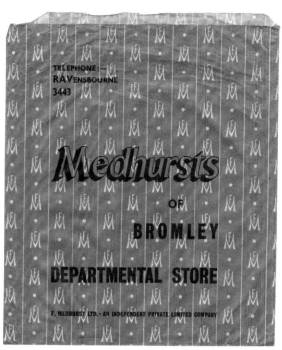

TELEPHONE :—
RAVensbourne
3443

Medhursts

OF

BROMLEY

DEPARTMENTAL STORE

F. MEDHURST LTD. - AN INDEPENDENT PRIVATE LIMITED COMPANY

MELODY CORNER

I do love a covered market. There's one in Tooting that's still going strong. Back in 1960, this little record shop opened up there selling chart hits and moving later into Irish music to cater for the large and enthusiastic local Irish community.

MEMRYDISCS

The name of this shop is a modern nightmare, as most spellcheckers or autocorrection apps will change it to what it sounds like – which is wrong. Yes, this single, long, badly spelled word was the name of a record shop in Hounslow. It operated throughout the 1960s until its building was demolished as part of a pavement-widening scheme.

MID ESSEX TELEVISION

It's all in the name really, and for once, we have a picture of the store that is now no more...

MIKE LLOYD MUSIC

Established in 1966, this shop was the epicentre of punk and new wave in the area, selling records, T-shirts and gig tickets, as well as organising travel for out-of-town events. After expanding into a megastore, it began to downsize, finally closing in 1998.

MILLER & HERD

From the blue and white candy-striped bag and that little bunch of records, this bag gives the impression of a lovely old emporium. Now it's a vape shop, called Dragon's Den, the Geek Vape Bar.

MJM

A pair of well-respected rock and pop shops that closed down in the noughties. What was the flagship store is now a branch of Subway.

AGAIN...
A RECORD!

MID ESSEX TELEVISION LTD.

BRANCHES AT—
BRAINTREE . MALDON . HALSTEAD . COLCHESTER

MIKE LLOYD MUSIC LTD

15 PERCY STREET, HANLEY
23 HIGH STREET, NEWCASTLE, STAFFS

MILLER & HERD

LIMITED

**33, THE PARADE
EXMOUTH**

Telephone 2043

Cassettes, Cartridges, Accessories

111 HIGH STREET   30 VICTORIA ROAD
NEW MALDEN   SURREY   SURBITON
Phone 01-949 4690   Phone 01-390 3106

MOONS

This 19th-century piano manufacturer and retailer was founded by Thomas Moon, a former choirboy. Their own pianos were not great quality, but very popular, and the company grew to be the largest of its kind in the UK. The shop expanded to include music lessons, sheet music, cabinet making, and a variety of other instruments. With the advent of sound reproduction a gramophone department was opened. The company was sold to J. F. Stone in 1963.

MORRIS

An early 78rpm jazz emporium – though this bag may come from the later period of selling knock-down vinyl. Not sure about the records and bicycles combination, but it's interesting to note the extremely early statement 'Records Bought'. We cannot think of an earlier bag on the tap for second hand goods.

MORTON'S

A well-respected jazz hangout with a host of jazz experts behind the counter. Now closed.

MUSICLAND

The first Musicland shop was established in Willesden Green in 1966 by Lee Gopthal, who also set up his own label, Pyramid Records. A friend and associate of Chris Blackwell, he helped to sell the R&B and reggae Blackwell and Island Records were introducing from Jamaica. Topped up with Top 40 pop, the shops rapidly expanded into areas with West Indian communities, also focusing on exciting American imports for vinyl-hungry West End geeks. Elton John worked behind the Soho counter for a time and Danny Baker was also on the staff. In 1968, Gopthal and Blackwell co-founded Trojan Records and by 1971 Musicland had expanded to over twenty shops. Some were later converted to Muzik City (see page 132), which concentrated on reggae, soul, calypso and selling the Trojan output. In 1972, Gopthal sold Musicland to the Ali family's Scene & Heard chain.

MUSIC EXPRESS

I do love a shop in an Underground station, such as the Baker Street branch of this small chain. As well as records, the owner hired Atari video-game cartridges to excitable youth.

MUSIC MARKET

This Oxford based chain was founded by Ian Howard, who went on to open the Borderline and Brixton Academy venues. The Music Market chain was sold on, expanded and eventually consumed by Our Price.

MUSICORE

This Durham shop, open throughout the 1970s and 1980s, also sold tickets to local gigs.

MUSICRAFT

Once a gift and record store in Surrey, now a sweetshop.

MUSICWISE

In addition to selling LPs and singles, this shop established in 1977, also ran a music lending library called Record Wise. After a fire at the premises, the shop moved up the road (in the direction the owl is pointing).

MUSICWISE LTD.

86 HIGH STREET - EGHAM - SURREY
Telephone: EGHAM 33400 & 36290

MUZIK CITY

This chain of stores owned by Lee Gopthal (see page 129) were located in mainly West Indian areas and sold reggae, caplypso and soul alongside much of the Trojan Records output. Declaring themselves 'the leaders in black music' in their advertisements, Muzik City forms an important link in the history of reggae music in the UK.

NAT'S RECORDS

Opened by Nat Fox (brother of Derek, see page 61), this pair of shops sold Jamaican music in London's East End.

NEMS

Epstein & Sons was a furniture shop owned by Harry and Queenie Epstein. They expanded into music, opening the North End Music Store, which was managed by their son, Brian. Under his stewardship, NEMS flourished into a small and successful chain, with three outlets in Liverpool and one in London. The Beatles were regular customers at the flagship Liverpool store and after recognising their talent, Brian placed them under contract – the rest of that story is well documented. After expanding into record production in the late 1960s, the shops closed in the early 1990s.

NOISES LTD

Possibly one of the best names in the book. And with such
a great name, it seems quite a surprise that everyone has
forgotten about the place.

Records and tapes

Nova Nova

**9 surrey street
littlehampton
telephone 3716**

LONSDALE PACKAGING—BRISTOL B/6

NOVA

I know it says 'Nova Nova' on the bag, but apparently it
was just called Nova and was a mod hangout.

NORRIS MUSIC CITY

72 GRANVILLE ARCADE
BRIXTON MARKET
S.W.9
TEL. 274/3727

AMERICAN AND JAMAICAN IMPORTS
ALWAYS IN STOCK

OLD
TOWN
RECORDS

63 HIGH STREET,
HEMEL HEMPSTEAD ☎ 55186

NORRIS MUSIC CITY

Self-proclaimed 'Reggae Soldier' Danny Norris was the manager of Music City Brixton, taking over when Trojan collapsed. The shop survived under his stewardship for another few years into the late 1970s.

ODDITY RECORDS

A well cool 1980s style, post-punk, futurist shop, located in the indoor market hall.

OLD TOWN RECORDS

Established in 1976 by classical-music enthusiast Arthur Grover, this double-fronted shop was situated in the 'old town' area of Hemel Hempstead. After Arthur sold up in 1983, the store carried on without him for a few more years.

OK RECORDS

This ambiguously named Kent shop had a good line in soul and jazz funk.

ODDITY RECORDS

Unit 2A & 3A
ON THE GROUND FLOOR
LEICESTER
INDOOR
MARKET
TEL 0533 516017

C.D.,TAPE,VINYL
bought sold
& exchanged
Posters & Memorabilia

ONE STOP

These fantastic and well-connected small Central London shops specialised in the import of rarities and promos. Famous customers included Jimi Hendrix, Mick Jagger and John Peel and this was also Danny Baker's first place of employment. After struggling to compete with the bigger and more aggressive Harlequin Records, the chain eventually folded in 1975.

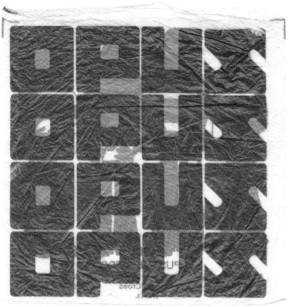

OPUS

This pretty cool small chain, manned by sophisticated staff, closed in the early 1980s following financial issues.

OXFAM

Founded in 1942, Oxfam is a confederation of several charitable organisations set up to alleviate poverty. Their first shop opened in 1949 in Oxford (initially called The Oxford Committee For Famine Relief, the name 'Oxfam' is the company's telegraphic address and was adopted in 1965). The reason Oxfam is included here is because – like all charity shops – this nationwide chain is a great place to go record hunting. Just a couple of weeks ago, I picked up the Third Ear Band's first LP (first UK pressing) for a fraction of the price it should have been. I mentioned in the introduction that charity shops usually didn't give away bags, but I have managed to find this 1970s one from Oxfam. Someone sure as hell lucked out with 'The Sound Of Music'.

OUR PRICE

This chain started life in 1971 as The Tape Revolution, selling popular music on cassette and 8-track formats. With growing demand for vinyl, in 1976 the company rebranded as Our Price. Following the purchase of Harlequin Records in the 1980s, the chain exploded. Expanding to more than 300 branches, it became the second-largest music retailer, behind Woolworths. After floating on the London Stock Exchange in 1984, the company was bought by WH Smith in 1986. WH Smith acquired the Virgin Music chain in 1994 and attempted to combine the two, which was when complications set in. As Virgin stores were opened, Our Price shops closed. A large number of Our Price stores were also rebranded as VShops, complete with modern shopping ideas such as instore electronic ordering terminals. This 'clicks and mortar' revolution failed and in 2001, the remaining seventy-seven Our Price stores were sold to the Australian company Brazin for just £2.

OZ

It's all in the pink bag. Everything. This late 1960s / early 1970s shop was situated in the Westgate Road area of Newcastle, known for its sexy leather and noisy bikes. Oz record shop was part of the scene, selling heavy metal and hard rock to the locals. Hell yeah. We can also tell you that it has absolutely nothing to do with *Oz*, the controversial counterculture magazine. But they did have a mobile disco you could hire.

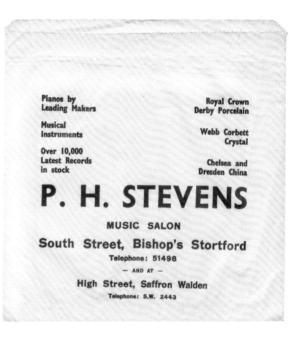

P & J RECORDS

Owned by chain-smokers Pauline and Don, this shop was an authorised chart vendor, so their weekly sales figures contributed to a record's position in the Top 100, etc. This meant that record reps were constantly turning up with new product, promos and white labels (records that were rarer than the standard-issue versions, often released just for DJs, with different labels, promotional stamps, or sometimes just blank white labels).

P.H. STEVENS

Today a Marks & Spencer occupies the small plot of high street that was once home to the Regent Cinema and the P.H. Stevens music shop, established in the 1920s by Percy Stevens, who was later joined by his brother Wilfred. Their neighbouring shops, one selling electrical appliances, the other glass and china, were soon amalgamated. With the advent of the rockin' 1950s, the crockery was moved upstairs to make way for a ground-floor music shop. It quickly became a popular hangout for music fans and musicians. The shop closed in the 1980s when the area was redeveloped. You can now buy a prawn sandwich where Ricky Valance once signed autographs.

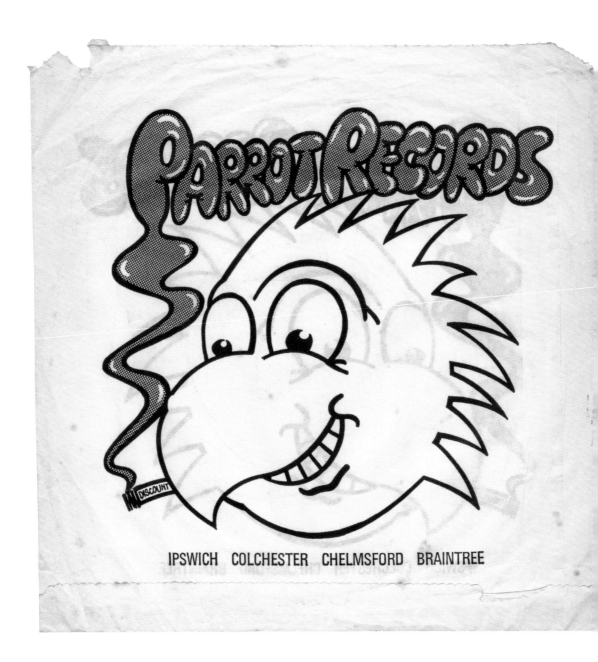

IPSWICH COLCHESTER CHELMSFORD BRAINTREE

PARROT RECORDS

This well-known and fondly remembered chain opened in 1982 and lasted for two decades, until the usual rent rises, increased competition and downloads led to its demise.

The smoking parrot on the bag was drawn by legendary artist Savage Pencil, real name Edwin Pouncey (see also Rough Trade and Zippo).

24 CAMBRIDGE HEATH ROAD·E.1. TEL. 790 1074

PAUL FOR MUSIC

Opened in 1954, over the next decade this shop became a reggae hot spot. The chain grew to three stores and two stalls, including the Leather Lane Music Shop. Paul retired in 1987 and the shops finally closed in 2005.

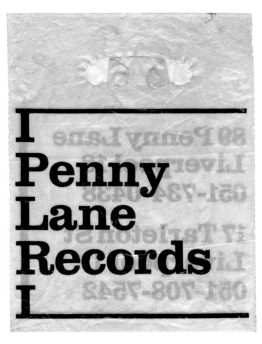

PECKINGS

Established by George 'Peckings' Price in 1960 to distribute Jamaican music in the UK. Initially selling vinyl from a suitcase he toted around the Ladbroke Grove area, in 1974 he opened a shop on Askew Road, Shepherds Bush. Price's best friend back in Jamaica was the famed producer Coxsone Dodd, so he pretty much had exclusivity when it came to the hot Studio One recordings. Now safely in the hands of Price's sons, the shop played an important role in the dissemination of Jamaican music across the UK. By the way, 'Peckings' refers to the rocking, chicken-like movement George made when dancing to the music.

PENNY LANE RECORDS

No prizes for guessing where this 1970s shop was located. Specialising in modern music and secondhand, the business outgrew its first premises and moved to larger ones, eventually expanding to three stores before closing in 1990.

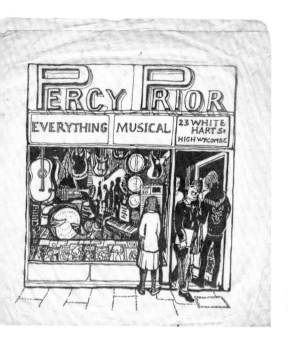

PEOPLE'S SOUND

This shop was established in 1988 by Von Barrington Adams – better known as Daddy Vego, the Jamaican legend, original 'Selector' and carnival stalwart. Set in the heart of Notting Hill, opposite the Mangrove Club, it's likely named after the 'Original People's Sound' sound system – the first static sound system he set up at one of the early carnivals. Vego died in 2016, but his name and shop live on.

PERCY PRIOR

After expanding his operation from a single outlet to two shops, Percy was forced to close one, before shutting down entirely.

PETER RUSSELL'S

Originally opening a jazz shop, Russell quickly realised how unpopular the genre was in his local area. He diversified into mail-order and hi-fi sales to survive, and after sonically educating the population of his home town, retired in 1992.

PHASE 1

An Essex record shop from the 1970s.

PLASTIC WAX

Bristol's longest-running record shop and possibly the biggest in terms of stock carried. It is still trading, but only from the one shop and with a bag far less cool than this one.

POP INN

Established by Ronnie Miller, this shop capitalised on the punk explosion, selling singles, LPs, torn T-shirts and bondage trousers. He later set up a backroom studio for indie bands to make killer videos. Cool.

POP-STOP

This bag, with its cartoon-style logo (a nod to a London bus stop, or Underground signage) carries all the information we could find on this former small chain.

PIC A-DISC

There is no record of this shop anywhere. But a few of these hand-stamped record sleeves have been found, for this and other shops. Dating from the late 1950s / early 1960s, these printed sleeves were sometimes just given away with jukebox purchases. So it's worth having an example of such things in this book.

I Get My Trax at

PLASTIC WAX

Bristol's Nº1 Collectors Record Shop

48 West Street
Old Market
Bristol 2
Tel. (0272) 558114

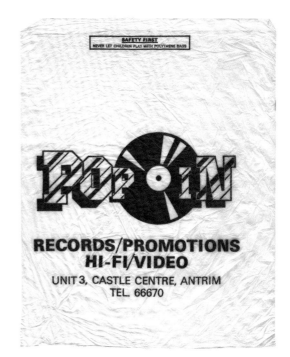

SAFETY FIRST
NEVER LET CHILDREN PLAY WITH POLYTHENE BAGS

RECORDS/PROMOTIONS
HI-FI/VIDEO

UNIT 3, CASTLE CENTRE, ANTRIM
TEL. 66670

POP INN
DISCOUNT RECORDS

11 BADDOW ROAD   BASILDON MARKET
CHELMSFORD, ESSEX ALSO AT (TUES. FRI. SAT.)
TELE: 59824

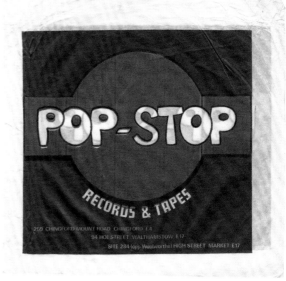

POP-STOP
RECORDS & TAPES

259 CHINGFORD MOUNT ROAD, CHINGFORD E4
94 HOE STREET, WALTHAMSTOW E17
SITE 284 (opp. Woolworths) HIGH STREET MARKET E17

150

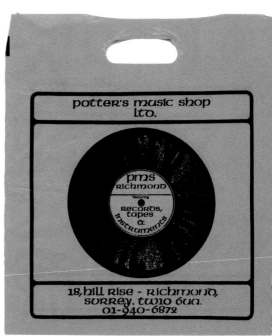

POTTER BROTHERS

I really like the incongruous imagery of this design: we have a gothic typeface on a worn-out ancient bag, then a modern pop soul diva and possibly a member of Bucks Fizz top left. All followed by the enchanting word 'Tenterden'.

POTTER'S MUSIC SHOP

This shop was established by drummer Ted Potter, who taught Elvis Costello to play guitar in the back room. He sold instruments as well as records and at one point had expanded to three shops, but it is unlikely the chain survived into the 1980s.

POTTERS

This shop was located just up the road from where I used to live: Aldershot, home of the British Army. Potters opened in 1810 and specialised in the manufacture of military drums – those fine painted ones seen at military tattoos being banged by the Blues and Royals. From my only visit in the early 1980s, I vaguely recollect a sad set of green racks with military-band and classical LPs.

PREEDY

This book, stationery and record shop served the Wolverhampton area from 1936 to 1979.

R. & B. RECORD SHOP

You might think this shop specialised in rhythm and blues, but you'd be very much mistaken. In 1959, Jewish couple Rita and Benny Ibsen (who later changed their name to King), opened the R. & B. Records Shop in Stamford Hill. They knew the local West Indian community wanted West Indian sounds, so that's what R & B supplied. They were quite possibly the earliest shop to sell reggae in the UK, and throughout the following decade, the premises were crammed full of young ska fans and mods. In the early 1960s, the area was a hotbed of 'new modernists', many coming from the Stamford Hill Boys And Girls Club. Members included Mark Feld (later to become Mark Bolan), Helen Shapiro and Alan Sugar. Rita and Benny also started their own label in 1963 (R. & B. Records), again one of the first to issue Jamaican music here in the UK. Releases included tunes by The Skatalites, Lee Perry, Tommy McCook, The Maytals, The Wailers and many more. They ended up with several other subsidiary labels too. By many accounts, Rita was a force to be reckoned with, regularly travelling to Jamaica to buy rights, tapes and records. The shop closed in 1984, but its importance in the nascent UK reggae scene cannot be ignored.

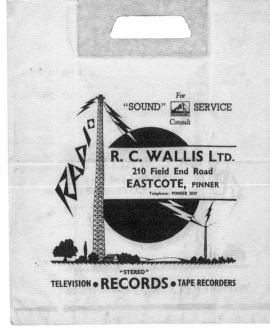

R.A.D.A.R.

Sad to say that this electrical appliance and music shop is on no one's radar at all.

R.C. WALLIS

What an electrifying bag. The shop is now a bar specialising in rum-based beverages.

RADIO & RECORDS

I would love to know what Mr Hoare bought for 3/5.

RADIOGRAM

There is no information to be found about this small shop in Essex with a cool name.

Ray's Jazz Shop

180 Shaftesbury Avenue,
London WC2H 8JS.
Tel: 01-240 3969

RAY'S JAZZ SHOP

This famous shop was started by Ray Smith when he took over Collet's jazz department (see page 56). Over the years, the triangular-shaped store, with entrances on both Monmouth Street and Shaftesbury Avenue, became a jazz mecca; its 'Rare As Hen's Teeth' auction box was always worth a flick. In the late 1990s, it expanded to incorporate a blues basement, but Ray was forced to sell up in 2002 after yet another rent increase. The shop is now part of Foyles on Charing Cross Road, but is a shadow of its former Shaftesbury self. I always had a bit of a problem with the cat's nose on that bag.

RAYNERS

This was a two-storey shop, with rock and pop upstairs and classical in the basement. The man in charge was called Ray and just about every account I've read paints him as an awful person. Ray also possessed a constantly wet and shiny face.

READINGS

The Station Approach shop was established around 1960 by John Readings, a jazz enthusiast. He bought pretty much anything that was pressed, so by the mid-1970s he had accumulated a mass of unsold 1960s stock. The construction of a larger tube-station entrance meant the demolition of the building and the shop moved to new premises in Lavender Hill. John retired in 1983 and the business was taken over by Citicenta Records.

RECKLESS RECORDS

This classic Soho store was established in 1984 and a Chicago branch in 1989: both are still going strong. In the early 1990s, their buyers made regular trips to the US, returning with underrated jazz, funk and soul LPs.

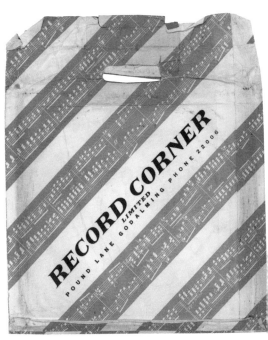

RECORD & TAPE CENTRE

Two mid-1970s shops, using the typeface from the *Record Collector* magazine on their bags.

RECORD COLLECTOR

Established in 1978 by Barry Everard and still open. This may well be down to Barry's super taste in the strange and obscure – whatever the reason, you rock Barry!

RECORD CORNER

First opened in 1958 to provide fine music to the people of Godalming and Surrey. And still doing just that!

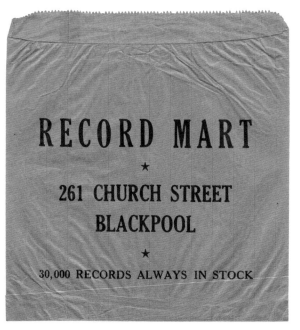

RECORD SAVINGS

NEW & SECOND HAND
RECORDS & TAPES
3 WHITE LION WALK
BANBURY (0295) 67378

SUNBURY TEL. 89300
STAINES TEL. 55125
ASHFORD TEL. 55322
Record Scene

RECORD SELECT

THE PLATT WADEBRIDGE CORNWALL

RECORD HOUSE

84 SYCAMORE ROAD, AMERSHAM, BUCKS, TELEPHONE AMERSHAM 3311
34 & 36 HIGH STREET, AYLESBURY, BUCKS, TELEPHONE AYLESBURY 80770
9 MARKET SQUARE, CHESHAM, BUCKS, TELEPHONE CHESHAM 78549
7A HIGH ST., PRINCES RISBOROUGH, BUCKS, TELEPHONE PRINCES R'BORO 6446

RECORD HUNTER

Established by John Goldsmith, a classical music enthusiast, with a young Harold Moores on the staff. Moores went on to take over the shop after Goldsmith founded Unicorn Records in 1968, a label that featured a classical repertoire alongside film music by greats such as Bernard Herrmann. Once Goldsmith was gone, the shop slowly moved on and then off. Moores eventually opened his own famous classical store in Soho.

RECORD MART

A popular Blackpool hangout, selling ex-jukebox singles and more. Known locally as 'Smokey Joe's' by virtue of the cigar-puffing owner.

RECORD RENDEZVOUS

Meet you there! It's now a healing and holistic centre, which (to me) is pretty much the same as a record shop really.

RECORD RETAILERS

I assume this was a group of small shops, joined under the Record Retailers banner, but with different shop names: Clapham Record Centre, Music Man, etc. We know that the Kilburn shop opened in 1961 and was sold to Harlequin in 1968. In addition, Harlequin took over the Strutton Ground premises of Music Man.

RECORD SAVINGS

This independent shop has been running for thirty years. Now, according to online sources, 'the pink pig is back', so perhaps it had closed down for a bit, or gone on holiday or something.

RECORD SCENE

Three shops that we know nothing more of.

RECORD SELECT

This shop (charming by all accounts) was based just outside the main thoroughfare of Wadebridge. It closed following online competition.

RECORD HOUSE

From what I can gather, this chain was opened by the Sinclairs, who had experience in the music business, having worked for various departments at EMI. The Amersham shop was on the premises of a former electrical goods and music shop called Radio House. This branch was eventually bought out by its manager, Graeme Campbell, and now trades as The Record Shop just up the road.

RECORDS & TAPES

This seaside record shop was open for at least two decades. I understand it closed at some point in the 1980s, just after they added 'Compact' to their name and got new purple plastic bags.

RECORDSVILLE

This important record mecca, not far from Victoria Station, was established in 1963 by Shaun Howard. It had a very nice sideline supplying records to London council libraries. It is best remembered as a punk hangout for The ASA (The Anarchist Street Army: a loose collective of angry schoolkids looking for trouble) and as an early adopter of those terrible manual credit card 'knuckle-buster' machine things. Shaun also owned Town Records (see page 210) as part of his business portfolio, but found two shops alongside the subsidiary library trading a bit of a handful. Closed in 1983.

REDIFFUSION

Established in 1928, this successful cable-TV and radio distributor branched out into several related areas, including broadcasting and retail. They established their own record label in 1968, with dedicated record centres, as well as selling records through their chain of high street electrical stores.

RED RECORDS

These Brixton and Peckham institutions closed in 2009. The Brixton branch is now a nail bar.

RECORDS
=&TAPES=

31 HIGH STREET - FALMOUTH
TELEPHONE 311936

BARCLAYCARD **Buy it with your Barclaycard**

CREDIT CARDS ACCEPTED
BARCLAYCARD
ACCESS
DINERS' CLUB

RECORDSVILLE
86-87 WILTON ROAD
VICTORIA SW1V 1DN
01-828 4825

ANOTHER RECORD FROM

REDIFFUSION

THE LATEST RECORDINGS
ALL MAKES STOCKED
DAILY ORDERING

THE RECORD CENTRE

6 MERCHANT STREET
BRISTOL - 1
Telephone 24606

4 FILWOOD BROADWAY, KNOWLE . . . Telephone 664869
6 THE HERMITAGE, HIGH STREET, SHIREHAMPTON Telephone 82-3589
63 GLOUCESTER ROAD . . . . Telephone 49045
156 WHITELADIES ROAD . . . . Telephone 33442

RED RECORDS
AND TAPES

TOP LP's and CASSETTES from £3.99
TOP 30 SINGLES from 98p
NEW 7" and 12" Singles — FAST

86 Rye Lane, Peckham, London SE15
Telephone: (01) 639 7980

RED RHINO

This independent label and associated groovy shops were launched in the late 1970s by husband-and-wife team Gerri and Tony K (Kostrzewa) as part of The Cartel – a small group of classic indie labels (including Rough Trade) that became a cooperative in order to get better distribution for their artists (such as The Smiths, The Cocteau Twins, Pigbag, etc). Red Rhino is the only shop in the book to have a tree growing on the inside. Opened in 1977, it closed in 1988.

REED

Opened in 1956 by Reg Reed, who also sold instruments and gave guitar lessons. After his death, the shop was run by his widow, Jean Reed (a woman with a fabulous memory for catalogue numbers). Fondly remembered for having a speaker attached to the wall outside so passers-by could hear what was playing inside. Closed down in the late 1980s.

REGIS RECORD CENTRE

For decades, a Hull hotbed of vinyl and musical accessories. Closed in the late 1980s.

REVOLVER

This important Bristol store, established by Roger Doughty (former owner of Driftin' Records), had no shop frontage as it was on the first floor. It had its own small label (Recreation) as well as independent distribution – it was part of The Cartel (see also Red Rhino and Rough Trade). Customers were often told to buy alternatives to their originally planned purchases, based on the owner's taste. This shop is indelibly linked to the rise of the 'Bristol sound', trip hop and Massive Attack. Closed down in the early noughties.

RHYTHM AGENCIES

Contrary to the modern-sounding name, this business was established pre-World War II to sell a range of instruments and records as well as tickets for classical concerts. Occasionally in the 1960s, a member of staff could be seen playing a Hammond organ in the shop window of the Reigate branch. It was still open in 1968, but I can't find any more information after that date.

RIPPING RECORDS

In 1975, John Richardson opened this much needed indie outlet in Edinburgh, also selling local gig tickets. It closed in 2016 when John retired.

RIVAL

A small but lively Bristol chain active through the 1970s and 1980s, eventually spreading into the city of Bath. I understand that the chain closed in the late 1980s but has recently been revived (in name and logo) as a new online record store, opened by a former work experience lad. Great news.

ROCK BOTTOM RECORDS

Established by Jim Hampshire in the 1960s, the shop was sold, to Mike Hoare, in 1985 and is still going strong, so much so he's just signed another five year lease. Jim Hampshire went off to start Canterbury Rock, another record shop still going strong.

ROLO

A large and popular record shop situated next to the fire station in Leyton, selling mainly pop. Closed in the late 1960s.

RON'S MUSIC SHOP

Yes, started in the early 1950s by Ron: he employed an assistant who was also called Ron, but was renamed Stan, to avoid confusion. Ron also had a Central London shop and both were piled high with rock, pop and classical records. The shops closed in 1974 when Ron (not Stan) died in the Ilford branch.

RONALDSONS

This shop, established in the 1950s, had its own recording studio.

ROCK BOTTOM RECORDS

THE LARGEST "ONE-MAN" RECORD SHOP IN THE WORLD

ROLO for RECORDS

368 LEA BRIDGE ROAD
LEYTON, E.10
LEYTONSTONE 4067

FIVE MILES OF RECORDS UNDER ONE ROOF

This record to be played at 45 r.p.m. with long playing stylus

YOUR FRIENDLY MUSIC SHOP

LEADING AGENTS FOR ALL
ENGLISH, CONTINENTAL & AMERICAN LABELS
STEREOPHONIC AND MONAURAL

Phone: ILford 2712

RON'S MUSIC SHOP
(ILFORD MUSIC SHOP LTD.)

WE ARE THE ONLY
SHOP IN THIS COUNTRY
SPECIALISING IN 45's

Why not come and browse through Our
Long Playing Department at Your Leisure
THOUSANDS OF L.P.s & E.P.s TO CHOOSE FROM

Pioneer Market, Ilford Lane, ILFORD
ESSEX

HiFi EQUIPMENT & 4
TAPE RECORDERS 5

Radio
Records
Music
Recording
Television

RONALDSONS
of
Southbourne

205, SEABOURNE RD.
Southbourne, BOURNEMOUTH
TELEPHONE : SOUTHBOURNE 1358

Visit our Recording Studio
Tape and Disc Equipment Installed

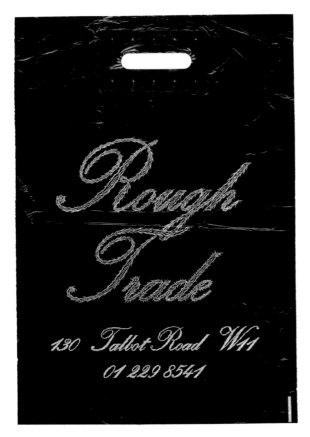

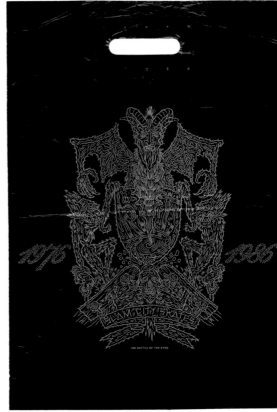

ROUGH TRADE

Established in 1976 by Geoff Travis in Kensington Park Road, the shop was apparently named after the Canadian new wave band, Rough Trade. The eponymous label started the following year, but was run as a separate entity from 1982, as the shops were bought out by the staff. The first shop moved to Talbot Road (where it still remains) and others opened in Covent Garden (now closed) and eventually Brick Lane (Rough Trade East), with additional branches abroad. The original shops were beacons of independent cool, radiating both weirdness and expertise. Currently somewhat more commercial, they still pack an almighty punch – hosting live shows as well as selling books (like this one) alongside secondhand vinyl. The bag shown opposite features artwork by Savage Pencil (see also Parrot and Zippo).

ROULETTE RECORDS

I like the uncluttered look of this bag. Thanks to the 'Sheffield Forum', I found out the shop was located in Rotherham. Dating from around the 1980s, it was likely killed off by the chain invasion.

ROUNDER

Started up in 1966, Rounder became an important part of the Brighton music scene, selling debut singles and gig tickets for local bands. Norman Cook aka Fatboy Slim worked there. Closed its doors in 2012, unable to make a profit against illegal file sharing, large online retailers and the recession.

RUMBELOWS

Opened in the late 1950s by Fred Dawes, whose eponymous chain of electronics retailers and rental shops was bought by Thorn (the electrical giant), along with another chain of electronic retailers called Sydney Rumbelow (see page 198). Thorn amalgamated the companies under the name 'Rumbelows'. Early incarnations of the shops had been selling records since their inception and the new chain continued to absorb other shops across the country (such as NEMS, see page 133). It is claimed that over its twenty-four years of trading, the legendary, ubiquitous chain of TV, radio and rental shops never actually made a profit. Looking back, they did seem a bit crap.

RUSHWORTHS

Established in 1828 by William Rushworth, who had grand ideas about his music shop, which by the mid-1950s was said to be the largest in Europe. It was here that Paul McCartney's dad bought him a trumpet, but fussy Paul wanted to sing and play at the same time, so it was all back to Rushworths to exchange it for a guitar. In 1963, Lennon and Harrison both bought imported Gibsons from the store. And of course, Rushworths sold records too. In 2002, after five generations of ownership, the store finally closed.

Ref. 3747

RUSSELL ACOTT

Established in 1811 by a Mr Russell as a small music shop, following the death of Russell the shop went to three partners: a botanist, a former mayor of Oxford (Frederick Ansell) and his son. By the 1950s, it had taken over another local music shop – Acotts. The newly named Russell Acott catered for all musical needs: piano hire, sheet music and of course the black crack that is vinyl. The shop closed down exactly two centuries after it had opened. The premises are now an All Bar One.

RYLANDS RECORD RENDEZVOUS

I couldn't find any information on this shop, but don't care because the bag is just THE BOMB.

S. NUTKIN

The last thing I was expecting to come across in this book was a squirrel. There's also an unexpected squirrel in *The Music Library* book. Sadly, I could find nothing more about this shop.

SAVE RECORDS

Opened by the Rochdale FC goalie Simon Jones in the late 1960s and spreading to four market stalls in halls across the surrounding area. The stalls finally closed in 2016 and stock is currently on line trading as DisCovery Records.

SAVILLE PIANOS

This chain of six shops was established in 1930. According to this bag, by the mid-1950s it was 'The Home of Music and Vision'. Unfortunately it isn't any more.

SCENE & HEARD

The 1970s chain owned by the Ali family. See also Musicland (page 129) and Muzik City (page 132).

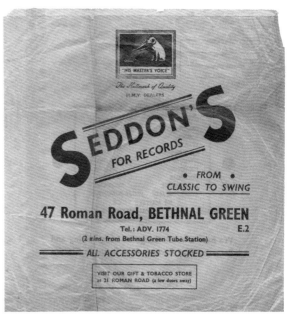

SCR ELECTRO SERVICES

Another small domestic appliances shop jumping on the vinyl bandwagon.

SEDDON'S

Apart from their other shop being a tobacconists, a few doors down, we know that Seddon's stocked just about every interesting label of the 1960s, including Vogue, Oriole, Regal Zonophone and all the other biggies.

198, NORTHOLT ROAD, & THE MARKET both opposite SOUTH HARROW station   tel 01·864·2622

SPECIALISTS IN NEW & SECONDHAND

RECORDS & BOOKS

sellanby

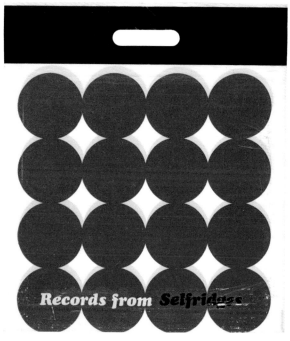

SELLANBY

The name was pronounced 'Sell and Buy' – which is exactly what the original stall in South Harrow did. Customers could buy and sell records and books, returning their purchases a few weeks later to get half the money back to spend on more. Established by Mr and Mrs Smith in the 1950s, the stall eventually expanded to two additional shops, with their sons taking over management. These well-loved emporiums survived into the late noughties, when the sons retired.

SELFRIDGES

Call Mayfair 1234 and order yourself something from one of the poshest record departments of all time. First opened in the 1950s, fellow high-end retailer Harrods also had a music department that was still trading until the 1970s. Then they realised more money could be made elsewhere.

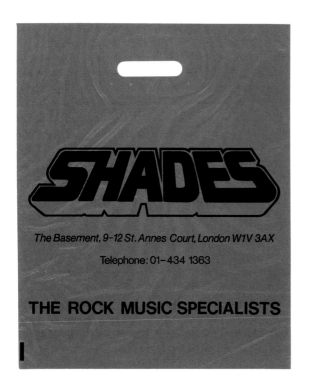

SHADES

Opened in 1978 by Mike Shannon, this was the heavy metal destination where bands came to meet fans and sign new LPs. It's also possible that the shop coined the terms 'thrash metal' and 'death metal' as they were first to sell these genres. They were also finding bands before anyone else, picking up tapes by Metallica before they were even signed. Shades stopped rocking in 1992, when the major labels moved in and the rock scene splintered into a thousand pieces.

SHAKESPEARE

This groovy shop was established by Gerald Shakespeare in the train station at Hull (originally named Paragon Station). It's likely to have been located in one of the building's beautiful traditional kiosks that have pretty much all now been destroyed.

SHERWINS

F.W. Sherwins was a large music and records store in Hanley, run by the Sherwin brothers, Gilbert and Roy. It had a large record department in the basement with several telephone-box style listening booths. The shop closed in the late 1970s.

SIFTERS

In the last verse of the Oasis song 'Shakermaker', Noel Gallagher wrote: 'Mister Sifter sold me songs when I was just sixteen'. And he's still selling people lots of songs – now thirty years in the business. Brilliant.

SMALL WONDER

This late 1970s shop and indie label were established by Pete and Mari Stennett. Their releases included music by Crass, The Cure and Bauhaus (including the legendary 12-inch of 'Bela Lugosi's Dead'). The shop is also name-checked in the Clash song 'Hitsville UK'. It closed down in the early 1980s, as racial tension in the area escalated.

SMITH'S OF WYMONDHAM

The best thing about this shop is that they owned a converted Ford Anglia van covered in bright slogans such as 'TV Rental' and 'we're on the ball for records', alongside the Pye logo and record sleeves stuck to its sides (this is back in 1961, by the way). Most importantly, the van had a giant HMV gramophone and Nipper the dog standing on the roof.

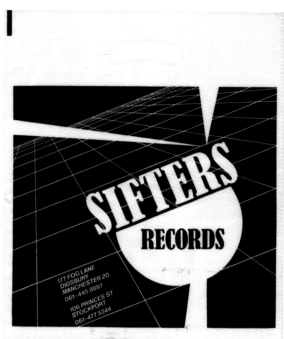

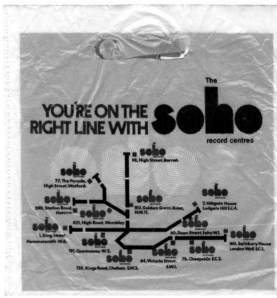

SOHO RECORDS

This shop on the corner of Dean Street was established by charismatic showman Alex Strickland in 1958, after he had successfully sold records from the backroom of a small tobacconist nearby. In 1960, he opened the Alex Strickland store, followed by a further fifteen shops in and around the city. The Soho Records Centre was visited regularly by showbiz stars, helping to sell huge amounts of LPs, and shop bags were often used as tickets to gigs. In 1965, Strickland sold a large share of the business to Pye Records and by 1970 Pye owned the business completely, slowly running it into the ground over the next few years.

Solent Music

THE RECORD CENTRE

30 WELLINGTON WAY, WATERLOOVILLE.
TELEPHONE: WATERLOOVILLE 51201

SOUNDCLASH RECORDS

28 St Benedicts Norwich 01603 761004

SOUND EFFECT

RECORDS & TAPES
THEATRE & CONCERT TICKETS
YORK TEL. (0909) 29962

Sound Ville RECORDS

78 CRAVEN PARK ROAD, LONDON, N.W.10
01-965 2269

SOUNDS GOOD RECORD CENTRE
368 LEA BRIDGE RD.
(MARKHOUSE CORNER)
LEYTON E.10
TEL: 539 4067

8 TRACKS ★ CASSETTES
STYLI ★ BATTERIES

Sounds Right
110 HIGH STREET WALTHAMSTOW. E.17
01-520 5128

SOUNDSVILLE RECORDS & TAPES
320 GLOUCESTER ROAD, HORFIELD, BRISTOL 7
Telephone: (0272) 427791

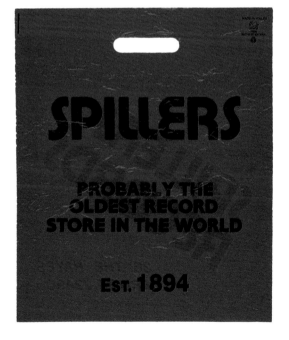

SPILLERS

PROBABLY THE
OLDEST RECORD
STORE IN THE WORLD

EST. 1894

SOLENT MUSIC

After a reasonable amount of research, I can confirm this shop was open in 1970 (I found a *Record Mirror* listing of shops selling records by The Groundhogs at that time).

SOUNDCLASH

This shop selling new and secondhand records opened in 1991 and is still going strong, three decades and three lockdowns later.

SOUND EFFECT

Started in 1970 by a twenty-two-year-old Nick Banks, this was York's first dedicated record shop. As well as the usual rock, pop and classical, Banks apparently spotted the rise of Northern soul and subsequently began to import singles from the US. The shop has now closed down, but it must surely be the only one in this book to have a bench dedicated to its memory (it's in King's Square if you're interested).

SOUND VILLE

This chain of shops were a hot spot for reggae and a major outlet for records on the Pama label. Some stores eventually became part of Muzik City (see page 132).

SOUNDS GOOD

There is very little information about this shop.

SOUNDS RIGHT

A groovy little shop, perfect for a dig about before a night at Walthamstow dogs. Changed its name to Cavern Records in the noughties, before closing down in 2012.

SOUNDSVILLE

Opening in the 1960s, this shop probably survived for twenty years on the best street in Bristol for buying and selling records.

SPILLERS

Established in 1894 in Queens Arcade, Cardiff, selling wax cylinders, phonographs and shellac discs, today Spillers is recognised by Guinness World Records as the world's oldest record shop (there are shops in this book that were established earlier, such as Mann's, but they no longer sell records). When rent increases loomed in 2006, the future of the shop looked uncertain, but it was saved thanks to campaigning locals, politicians and rock stars. And yes, the shop rocks.

SPIN-A-DISC

This fun little record shop lasted until the local council bulldozed the entire area to build one of those homogenised retail parks.

SPIN IT

These two groovy little stores were formerly branches of Muzik City. The Willesden shop was situated close to Morgan Studios and was often frequented by famous hairy rockers getting some air.

SPINADISC

This lively and much missed Northampton shop opened in 1973 and shut down in the 1990s. It was recently revived as an online business by two ex-staff members. Good story.

SPINNING DISC

This is the shop I mentioned in my introduction that I couldn't remember the name of: Spinning Disc. A rarely open, teeny-weeny shop, crammed full of 1950s music – Elvis, Doo-Wop, Rockabilly, etc. Terry, the owner, knew everything about the era – musically at least. The shop closed down when Terry died, around 2012.

Telephone 01-892 3507

All Leading Record
Companies

COLOUR T.V.

HI-FI SALES
& SERVICE

STEREO SYSTEMS

DISCO SUPPLIES

T. V. RENTALS

553 Ivy Bridge Shopping Centre · Twickenham Road · Isleworth · Middx

SPIN IT

13 HIGH ROAD · WILLESDEN · N.W. 10
TEL. 459—0761

8 PARSON STREET · HENDON · N.W. 4

SPINADISC (RECORDS)
19A ABINGTON SQUARE,
NORTHAMPTON.
PHONE: 31144.

GOLDEN OLDIES
1950 - 1970

54 HIGH ROAD CHISWICK W4 1SZ · LONDON (UK)
TELEPHONE 0181-951 4606 · FAX 0181-568 8379

SQUIRE

This well-established musical instrument and electrical-repair shop had a record department in the basement. Most importantly, this is where a young, pre-fame Dusty Springfield worked. The shop and its partner store, Brendon's of Beaconsfield, were eventually sold to Curry's, but not before it was used to film scenes for an episode of *Minder*.

STARTIME

A small Essex-based chain, established in the 1960s, with a finger firmly on the pop pulse. The chain closed down in the mid-1980s.

STERN'S AFRICAN RECORD CENTRE

Stern's began in the 1950s as a modest Bloomsbury electrical retailer, unusually selling African music in the back room. In 1983, the lease ran out and the owner retired, so former members of staff decided to open Stern's African Record Centre directly behind the original shop. At the same time, they started a label and distribution network for African sounds. The shop was ultimately killed off by rent rises and the internet, but continues online as one of the largest and most important distributors of African music.

STEPHEN SIGER

A pair of shops active in the early 1980s.

STEVE'S SOUNDS

This great double-fronted store was located in a small alleyway between Leicester Square and Chinatown, with boxes of vinyl spilling into the street and a man on a stool guarding it all. Its large, unpredictable stock of secondhand and new vinyl was always worth a late-night dig. Opened in the 1970s, closed down in the early noughties.

STRAWBERRY FIELDS

Radio celebrity Tony Blackburn cut the ribbon to open this shop in the early 1960s. After surviving three changes of address and several changes of fashion (it even had a Battlezone arcade game at one stage), it failed to make it through the 1980s. This bag obviously once held an Osmond record.

STONE'S

A groovy old bag from the late 1950s. Sadly the shop has disappeared without a trace.

STEPHEN SIGER

Records ————

———— *Cameras*

LANSON HOUSE
HITCHURCH LANE
DGWARE, Middx.
ELEPHONE 01-952 8166

113 CRICKLEWOOD BDY.
LONDON, N.W.2
TELEPHONE 01-452 3593

AFRICAN RECORD CENTRE

116 WHITFIELD ST. LONDON W1
01-387 5550

STEVE'S SOUNDS

20 NEWPORT COURT
(NEAR LEICESTER SQUARE STATION)

LONDON W.C.2

*BIG DISCOUNT ON NEW LP's
CASSETTES & COMPACT DISCS
ALSO LARGE SELECTION OF
SECOND HAND LP's*

———— TEL.071-437 4638 ————

V. A.T. no. 241-741-874

Strawberry Fields

PENN PLACE RICKMANSWORTH
TELEPHONE 77894

STYLUS

A great polythene bag for a popular chain of 'record parlours', immediately conjuring up images of Formica bars, listening booths and milkshakes. But I think that this is actually a small group of internal Stylus retail booths set up in several larger shops (such as Weston Hart) along the south coast.

STUDIO MUSICA

This late 1960s and 1970s chain of shops sold sheet music and records across the Midlands, eventually expanding to five outlets. It closed down in the early 1980s.

SUBWAY

A small South of England chain with branches in Guildford, Basingstoke and Southampton. Good punky rocky shops – but a liitle intimidating if you were only eleven in 1972.

SUNDOWN

A small chain of 1970s discount record centres that moved premises because of redevelopment. They stopped selling records when video came along, and had all disappeared by the 1980s.

SUNSHINE RECORDS

ALL THE LATEST

POP, REGGAE, SOUL, AMERICAN, ENGLISH
and
WEST INDIAN RECORDS

MUSIC FOR ALL   ULTIMATE STEREO PRESENTATION

SUNSHINE RECORDS
31a, WESTBURY AVENUE,
WOOD GREEN, N.22.
(Opposite Turnpike Tube Station)
Tel. : 01-889 1156

GREEN SHIELD stamps

GET IT AT

Superdisc

BRANCHES AT

HERNE HILL Tel. 274-7046   WEST NORWOOD Tel. 761-2292
CATERHAM Tel. 48760   SELSDON Tel. 651-0383
MAIDSTONE Tel. 670679

FOR ALL YOUR RECORDS, TAPES & ACCESSORIES

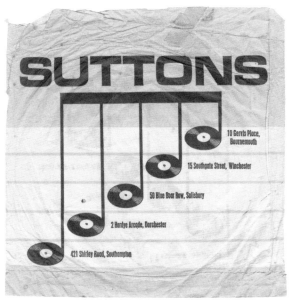

SUTTONS

10 Gervis Place, Bournemouth

15 Southgate Street, Winchester

50 Blue Boar Row, Salisbury

2 Hardye Arcade, Dorchester

421 Shirley Road, Southampton

SWALES MUSIC CENTRE

2, 4 and 6
HIGH STREET
HAVERFORDWEST

SYDNEY RUMBELOW

BRANCHES THROUGHOUT HERTFORDSHIRE

RADIO, TELEVISION, ELECTRICAL & MUSICAL SERVICES

SYDNEY SCARBOROUGH

record
& tape
centre

SYDNEY SCARBOROUGH LTD RECORDS & TAPES
UNDER THE CITY HALL · HULL · TELEPHONE 20515

RECORDS

STEREOCASSETTES
STEREO & CARTRIDGE TAPES

SIXTY YEARS OF SOUND SERVICE

SYDNEY
SCARBOROUGH LTD.

UNDER THE CITY HALL · HULL
TELEPHONE 20515

SYDNEY SCARBOROUGH LTD RECORDS & TAPES
UNDER THE CITY HALL HULL TELEPHONE 20515

SUNSHINE

I visited the site of this retailer recently – a tiny shop near Turnpike Lane tube in North London. I could find out nothing else about it, apart from the fact that it sold pop, reggae and soul back in the 1960s.

SUPERDISC

Another small chain with shops across South-East England.

SUTTONS

John Sutton established his first shop in 1949, after being demobbed. Starting out selling hardware, he got slowly more involved with music and in 1950 was the first shop in his area to stock the new-fangled 'LP'. As his business grew, so did his marketing methods. He developed the famous local 'listening panel', a wall with push buttons and earphones where customers could listen to a selection of the latest records. He also opened a music library. The chain closed in 1995 when Sutton retired.

SWALES MUSIC CENTRE

Joffre Swales and his wife Nan opened this outlet at the start of Beatlemania. The small shop expanded rapidly thanks to pop music advice from their three children, who watched *Juke Box Jury* religiously every week. Two of the siblings continued to run the shop until 2006, when online buying and the discount purchasing power of major chains brought it to an end, after forty-five years of trading.

SYDNEY RUMBELOW

Talented violinist Sydney Rumbelow opened his first shop in 1949, selling all things music and radio, as well as dabbling in the nascent television market. After considerable expansion, in the late 1960s he sold his chain of shops to Thorn. The shops were grouped with other chains purchased by Thorn (see Rumbelows page 171) and all renamed 'Rumbelows'. Meanwhile, Sydney left the corporate world behind and started another music shop which he ran until his death in 1974.

SYDNEY SCARBOROUGH

Established by Sydney Scarborough at the turn of the 20th century, this shop was to become a musical institution in Hull. With the growth of recorded sound, it began to sell gramophones and shellac records. The shop continued to embrace new technologies, installing listening booths in the 1950s. In the 1960s and 1970s, the record department was expanded, becoming a popular haunt of local teenagers (all overseen by the formidable Mr John). The shop finally closed down in 2001. There have since been a number of local exhibitions celebrating its long life and influence.

TANSLEY & COOKE

A medium-sized electrical chain in the South of England, that sold records alongside radios and televisions. The company ran an interesting set of advertisements in the 1960s, using old folk illustrations to talk about modern electronics. Closed down in the 1980s.

TELEFUSION

With a stake in Yorkshire Television, this large Blackpool-based chain of TV-rental and music shops was prominent throughout the 1960s and 1970s. Its flagship Blackpool store boasted a lively record bar and other outlets were spread across the UK, from Llandudno to Hastings. The business was bought by TV-rental company Visionhire in 1987.

TESCO

I'm pretty surprised Tesco have made it into the book, but from the evidence supported by this odd bag, they were trying to sell vinyl hit records back in the 1970s and 1980s. At one stage they did have their own discount record department, called Delamare, that sold cheap deadstock imports and cutouts. 'Sounds' may well have been a new sharper and more suitable incarnation once they realised Delamare was a tricky word.

THE 78 RECORD EXCHANGE

Established in 1963 by two 78rpm enthusiasts, Mr Kloet and Mr Howarth, as an extension of their shellac-collecting habits. Originally open only on Saturdays, high demand forced them to extend their hours. They also stocked standard 33s and 45s. Closed for business in 1996.

For the largest selection of Records

TANSLEY & COOKE LTD
BRANCHES AT BOGNOR REGIS · WORTHING · LITTLEHAMPTON
HORSHAM · STORRYS, CHICHESTER

RECORDS
Telefusion
THE BEST SELECTION IN TOWN

46 MOSTYN ST.,
LLANDUDNO

6 CONWAY RD.,
COLWYN BAY

TELEVISION·
STEREO AND
RADIOGRAMS · TAPE-RECORDERS·
RECORD-PLAYERS & TRANSISTORS·
TELEFUSION - THE CENTRE FOR HOME ENTERTAINMENT

TODAYS Sounds

TODAYS **TESCO**

THE **78** RECORD EXCHANGE

9 LOWER HILLGATE · STOCKPORT · CHESHIRE

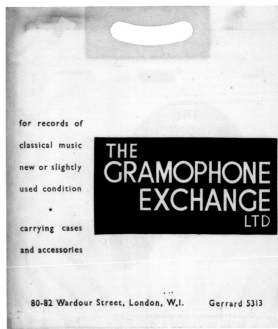

THE DISKERY

I absolutely love this shop in Birmingham. I remember sending a letter to them in the early 1990s asking them to keep an eye out for a particular British jazz LP. They called me two weeks later and told me one had 'just walked through the door'. Established by Morris Hunting in 1952, the shop still thrives. Apparently, this is the second oldest surviving record shop in the UK, after Spillers.

THE GRAMOPHONE EXCHANGE

The earliest mention I can find of this shop is from the 1940s, when apparently it was quite a destination (if you were into rare gramophone records and classical music). For me, it was always the last port of call if I was looking for an obscure film score and no one else knew what I was talking about. When the shop was about to die in 1991, one of the staff took over the concession, renaming it Gramex and relocating from Wardour Street to Lower Marsh (behind Waterloo Station). There it nestled, just getting increasingly strange, with snoring, dribbling old men asleep in button-back chairs on the ground floor and incredible jazz collections in the basement. It closed down in 2019.

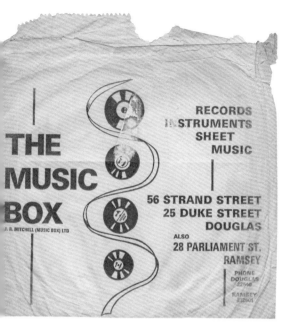

THE MUSIC BOX (Douglas)

The only Isle of Man record-shop chain store as far as I'm aware. I've no doubt that one of their biggest customers was a local man named John Peel (no, not that one), whose collection of more than fifty thousand LPs was sold in 2020. He must have got them somewhere.

THE MUSIC BOX (Erdington)

This musical instrument and record store was established in the 1950s by Mrs Fisher and Mr Davis. I understand they emigrated to Australia in the mid-1970s.

THE MUSIC BOX (Stoke Newington)

This well-stocked shop was established in the early 1960s by music fan Ken Mills. It's now a butcher that has a sausage competition every year.

EMI

CBS
RCA
DECCA
POLYDOR
and all other leading mkes....

THE MUSIC CENTRE

62 DALRYMPLE STREET

GIRVAN

RECORDS · MUSIC CASSETTES · 8 TRACK CARTRIDGES

THE MUSIC CENTRE

11 FORE STREET
KINGSBRIDGE
Tel 2576

Records · Tapes · Musical Instruments
Specialists in Stylus Care and Replacement

RECORDS

the **music hall**
record specialists

LPs

45s

11 Kingston Road
Wimbledon
S.W.19
CHErrywood 3750

ERX

THE MUSIC ROOM

8a MONSON ROAD
TUNBRIDGE WELLS
Telephone 32087/35076

2 QUARRY HILL ROAD
TONBRIDGE
Telephone 357479

CASSETTES & CARTRIDGES ● RECORD ACCESSORIES

RECORDS

THE MUSIC CENTRE (Girvan)

This shop in the small Scottish burgh of Girvan is now a tattoo parlour called Byeohazard.

THE MUSIC CENTRE (Kingsbridge)

This shop in Devon survived for at least a couple of decades.

THE MUSIC HALL

Established in the 1950s, this shop had a speaker outside so passers-by could hear the latest LPs and 45s.

THE MUSIC ROOM

The Tunbridge Wells shop was originally called McCowans Record Shop. The Music Room sold singles upstairs with listening booths at the rear. Its dimly lit basement, complete with psychedelic oil wheel, had a further two listening booths and smelled of damp and incense: magic.

THE MUSIC SHOP (Blackheath)

Established by Jean Williams in 1957, the shop was sold on to loyal staff member Doris Rome in the early 1960s. A classic local store selling rock, pop and secondhand records into the late 1970s.

THE MUSIC SHOP (Hailsham)

In the 1960s, this small music shop was located in the newly built Hailsham precinct.

THE RECORD BAR

This Lewes shop measured about 8ft by 8ft and was possibly the smallest record store in the UK with standing room for only two or three people at a time. It was demolished in 1970.

THE RECORD CASE

I have the distinct feeling this was a classical music shop, but I'm not certain. What I am sure of is that the 'New Boots and Panties!!' album cover photograph was taken outside the shop eleven doors down from this one on Vauxhall Bridge Road.

THE RECORD CENTRE (Sidcup)

A 1960s Sidcup record rendezvous that also sold sweets.

THE RECORD CENTRE (Tooting)

A lovely bag for what was apparently a good shop throughout the post-war years. It closed down sometime in the early 1980s: the premises is now a Starbucks.

THE RECORD CHEST

Harold Hill's most modern record shop is no longer.

THE RECORD CORNER

This small shop, operating throughout the 1970s and 1980s, sold funk, soul, Northern soul and disco. If you couldn't make it to Balham they also had a mail-order service.

THE RECORD FORUM

A lively shop that opened in 1956 and surprisingly changed its name in 1973 to Treble Clef (see page 210). The shop began dealing in secondhand stock from 1981. It sold out and became Sound Store before closing in the early 1990s.

THE RECORD PEDDLER

Specialists in Bowie as well as rock and new wave throughout the 1980s. Also a good line in Factory Records rarities thanks to connections with Factory staff and fans. Closed in 1992.

THE RECORD SCENE

This chain of four stores was also the global headquarters for the Cliff Richard and The Shadows Fan Club. By contrast, the shops were major retailers of punk and new wave, even starting their own label, Scene Records, which released just one single. Although they closed down in the early 1980s, I believe the fan club is still thriving.

THE RECORD SHOP (Bath)

No information could be found about this shop.

Extensive Stocks Of Records To Suit All Tastes

THE RECORD FORUM SYD. 3905

56, SYDENHAM RD., S.E.26

Record Carrying Cases
Storage Cabinets & Racks
Recording Tapes
Pre-Recorded Tapes
Complete Range of Styli
Sheet Music

A WIDE RANGE OF CASSETTES & CARTRIDGES IN STOCK

The Record Scene

Branches at

ASHFORD
TEL. 55322

STAINES
TEL. 55125

SUNBURY
TEL. 89300

CHERTSEY
TEL. 61697

The **RECORD SHOP**

Proprietors:
WESSEX LIBRARIES Ltd

13 SOUTHGATE STREET • BATH
TELEPHONE 66945

JERSEY'S LARGEST AND MOST POPULAR RECORD STORE

THE RECORD SHOP

19 QUEEN STREET, ST. HELIER.   CENTRAL 21522

66 Fife Road
Kingston

THE RECORD SHOP

01 546 3880

CIVILITY AND SERVICE GUARANTEED
The Biggest Little Record Shop in Town

★ ALL MAKES OF RECORDS AVAILABLE ★

★ GREETINGS CARDS FOR ALL OCCASIONS ★

BOOK YOUR TICKETS HERE FOR ALL LONDON THEATRES, CONCERTS AND SPORTING EVENTS

"THE SPINNING DISC"

6 BRIDPORT HOUSE, FORE ST., EDMONTON, N.18

Tel. EDM. 7555

A LARGE RANGE OF TAPES, PLUGS, STYLI AND ACCESSORIES ALWAYS IN STOCK

THE TURNTABLE

AGENTS
FOR ALL LEADING
MAKES OF TRANSISTOR
RADIOS, TAPE RECORDERS Etc.

210 KING STREET
HAMMERSMITH
LONDON, W.6.
01-748 2534

AND

1 CORNER HOUSE PARADE
EPSOM ROAD
EWELL, SURREY
01-393 1881

THE RECORD SHOP (Jersey)

A large record shop occupying a spacious corner plot in St Helier's main shopping street. Having searched the Jersey archives, it appears that the site was commercially redeveloped in 1983, which can only mean one thing.

THE RECORD SHOP (Kingston)

This retailer of secondhand records and CDs opened in the late 1970s and closed in the late 1990s.

THE SPINNING DISC

This North London shop used to open on Christmas Day, so everyone who had been given record tokens could spend them immediately.

THESE RECORDS

This 'art' record shop was essentially someone's front room near Vauxhall. It was run by two brothers, one of whom was Howard, who I met though the radio station Resonance FM. His show was called *The Bermuda Triangle*, a name that could easily have applied to this shop: once you entered, you got the feeling you might never emerge. There was always some kind of an installation inside, like a bathtub full of CDs, or the Twin Towers constructed from CD jewel cases. Like a variation on the Dead Parrot Sketch, staff might well attempt to argue you out of buying their obscure recordings: nothing was normal here, especially not the conversations. Anyone who ventured in would always remember the experience. A brilliant shop, now closed.

THE TURNTABLE

No information could be found about these shops either.

THORPE'S RECORD BAR

This seems to be half travel agent and half record shop ('Can I have a Midnight Train to Georgia'?) I have read that Mrs Thorpe, the proprietor, gave away records she couldn't sell to young kids who came into the shop.

THRESHOLD

Opened in 1972, this shop was situated in a modern shopping precinct. It was named after the Moody Blues LP 'On the Threshold of a Dream' and members of the band were on hand at the shop's opening. The shop survived until the early 1980s, but is now a branch of Sports Direct.

TIPPLE OF PECKHAM

This shop opened in the 1950s as a newsagent that also sold toys and later, vinyl. To view the records it was necessary to make an appointment and the singles had a string though the middle so they couldn't be stolen. Apparently, Mr Tipple got bored of records and stopped selling them. Years later, he decided to get rid of all his deadstock (ska, jazz and more, now thirty years old and still unplayed) from the basement, selling it for around £5 a record (pre-internet of course). Sadly, Mr Tipple was mugged in his own shop, which was probably a contributing factor to his closing down.

TOWER RECORDS

This small indie chain offered a glimmer of excitement for bored teenagers in a number of fairly dull towns throughout the 1970s and early 1980s. Nothing to do with Tower Records, the monster American global chain that went bankrupt (for the first time) in 2004.

TOWN RECORDS

Established by Shaun Howard, who also owned Recordsville (see page 162), this cool 1960s shop was the place for all things hip, proggy and underground. Mick Jagger and Bill Wyman would leave Keith Richards asleep in the shop's armchair in the morning, coming back to collect him at the end of the day.

TRACKS

A small chain of three stores that closed down in 2005.

TREBLE CLEF

Formerly The Record Forum (see page 206), which opened in 1956. Renamed as the Treble Clef in 1973 when the shop changed hands. Continued trading until the late 1980s.

CAMERASPORTS
West Byfleet 41598
Surrey

TOWER RECORDS
20 High Street
Walton 42792 Surrey

TOWER RECORDS
LEISURETIME
WEST BYFLEET
49375

TOWER RECORDS
11 High Street
Leatherhead 73684 Surrey

TOWER RECORDS
35 High Street
Camberley 61866 Surrey

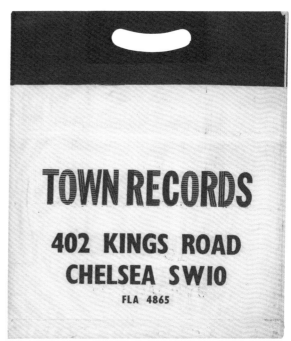

TOWN RECORDS
402 KINGS ROAD
CHELSEA SW10
FLA 4865

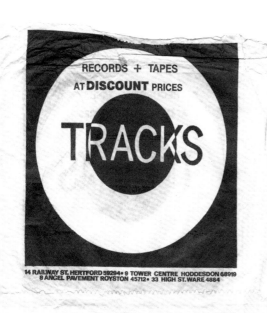

RECORDS + TAPES
AT **DISCOUNT** PRICES

TRACKS

14 RAILWAY ST. HERTFORD 59294 • 9 TOWER CENTRE HODDESDON 68919
8 ANGEL PAVEMENT ROYSTON 45712 • 33 HIGH ST. WARE 4884

Treble Clef

Records & Tapes
56 Sydenham Road Sydenham London SE26

TUDOR RECORDS

418 · MUSWELL HILL BROADWAY · 883·0674

TUDOR

Run by Jean and Wilf (aka 'Bunny') Gold, the shop was named after the local area dialling code, which was TUD. They carried a great selection of stock and guaranteed to get in anything you wanted to order. The Golds retired and sold the shop on to Alan Davison. It is now an estate agent.

TURNER ELECTRICAL

This 1950s electrical shop also rented televisions and sold records. Note that busy little bell boy...

"More Records from

Turner Electrical Ltd.

KING STREET   CHAPEL STREET

BRIDLINGTON   Tele.: 4775

MURRAY STREET

FILEY   Tele.: 3122

TW RECORDS

This small chain of stores was established by Ray Sams in 1965. The shops had records in the front and a café out the back. Although TW stands for Twisted Wheel, I don't believe the shops were heavily into the Northern soul side of things. The Erith shop was the last to shut down, in 2005.

UNLIMITED SOUND

The first set of shops I've come across that claim they actually made their own stereo equipment.

6 ST. GEORGE'S STREET, WINCHESTER, HANTS. 0962 63261

26/27 DOWNING STREET, FARNHAM, SURREY. 0252 723566

5/6 THACKERAY MALL, FAREHAM SHOPPING CENTRE, FAREHAM, HANTS. 0329 237231

VALLANCES

Established in 1934 by Alec Vallance, selling the usual electrical goods and services alongside music and music related gear. At their peak, this chain consisted of around forty shops, mainly in the North of England. There were many celebrity openings, with *Coronation Street* stars and radio DJs cutting the ribbons on new stores during the 1960s. The company was sold by Vallance's son in 1987.

VENUS

This shop in Farnham was very near the Sainbury's that started me on the whole 'Own Label' book trip. Not sure what happened in the end. Maybe they went to sell records on another planet.

VICKERS-OWEN

There is no information about this old shop but that is offset by the fact that the bag has a really great fade. Lovely how that green is going slightly orangey gold.

VINYL EXCHANGE

Opened for business in 1988, selling old and new records, tapes and CDs. Still going strong.

VINYL VILLAGE

Opened by talented guitarist and band manager Kris Gray in 1984. Quite short-lived as Gray had bigger fish to rock out with.

VINYL ZONE

The most important component of this long-disappeared shop was one of the counter staff, Jazzy M (real name Michael Schiniou). He was a charismatic salesman and radio DJ who relentlessly promoted jazz-funk, soul, dance and the burgeoning house sound of the late 1980s. An important go-to London store for just about every pirate and early house DJ.

VICKERS-OWEN
The Record Shop ≡ LTD.

Stockists of Radio-Grams & Hi-Fi of
H.M.V., Ferguson, Marconiphone & Ultra

───────

TAPES, CASSETTES & CARTRIDGES

───────

12 MILL STREET · WHITCHURCH · SHROPSHIRE

(TELEPHONE 2609)

RECORDS · TAPES · C.D.'S.

Vinyl

exchange

18 OLDHAM ST · MANCHESTER CITY CENTRE ☎ 061-228-1122

BOUGHT · SOLD · EXCHANGED

Produced from DEGRADABLE film: decomposes harmlessly in soil

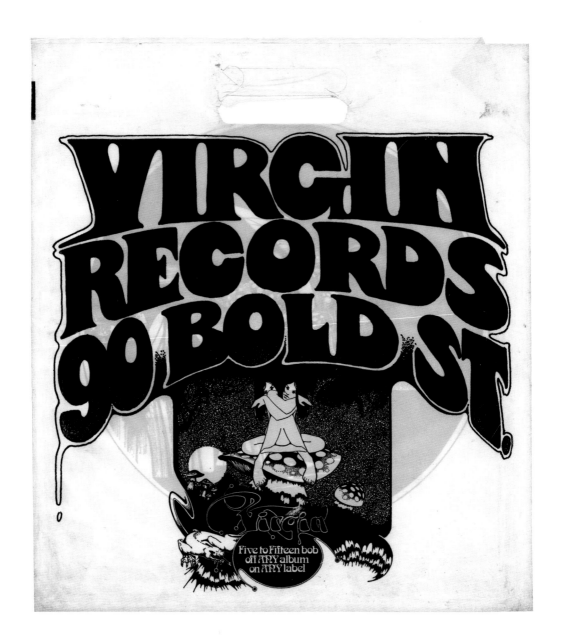

VIRGIN RECORDS

Established as Virgin Records and Tapes by Richard Branson and Nik Powell in 1971, the first shop, located in Notting Hill Gate, sold Krautrock and gave away vegan food. A proper store in Oxford Street quickly followed, and the empire expanded rapidly thanks to the success of the Virgin Records label, with the first megastore opening in 1979. I remember visiting one of the megastores in the 1990s: there was a life-size cut-out of Richard Branson with a lot of rude things scrawled all over it, especially on his face. Roger Dean (probably most famous for his Yes album covers) designed the Virgin logo in 1972 and was responsible for the classic figurative-fantasy bag artwork.

137 The Moor
Sheffield Tel 70929

VĬRGIN RECORDS

VISIRAD

There's something strangely pleasing about the name of this old shop.

W.G.

W.G. Stores was a shop and record stall in Shepherd's Bush Market. Opened in the 1950s, it survived into the 1970s. The shop supplied the records for the half-time playlist at nearby Queens Park Rangers Football Club. It may have moved into hardware after record sales dwindled in the 1980s.

WALL OF SOUND

The unstoppable collector Elliot Smaje decided to consolidate his love of music and books by opening a market stall in 1986. This turned into a shop, which, after a number of incarnations, is now housed in the basement of Crash Records in Leeds.

WALLY FOR WIRELESS

Founded by Wally Segal in 1955, the shop was opened by superstar of the time Frankie Vaughan ('Mr Moonlight'), causing a small stampede in the process.

WATKINS FOR RECORDS

This small Tooting market stall was opened in 1949 by the Watkins brothers – Charlie and Reg. After moving to a shop in Balham and getting into instrument sales and manufacture, they developed The Watkins Copicat (1958). This legendary echo unit, designed primarily for use with guitar, revolutionised music overnight and is still in production today.

WAX RECORD CENTRE

This groovy small chain dealt in the usual rock and pop, but their main selling point (which they regularly advertised) was their ability to order and import obscure soul.

WESTON HART

This shop was established after the war by Vera Leek to sell and service wireless sets for dockers and sailors in Portsmouth. The coronation of Elizabeth II in 1953 launched an explosion in television sales, something that Vera capitalised on. She also opened a record department at the rear of the store. In the mid-1960s, she handed the business to her daughters, Mary and Jill. The business grew throughout the 1960s and early 1970s, expanding to eleven branches by 1975. The company was sold to the electrical retailer Woolacotts in the same year.

Wells
Music
Stores

ORGANS *PIANOS *MUSICAL INSTRUMENTS *RADIO *TV *GRAMOPHONE RECORDS *DOMESTIC *
BRANCHES THROUGHOUT ROMFORD

WELLS MUSIC STORES

Established by Arthur Wells in the early 1960s and fondly
known as WMS, this shop expanded to a handful of stores
in and around the Romford area. Arthur's son took over
the running of the business before the chain eventually
closed in 1996.

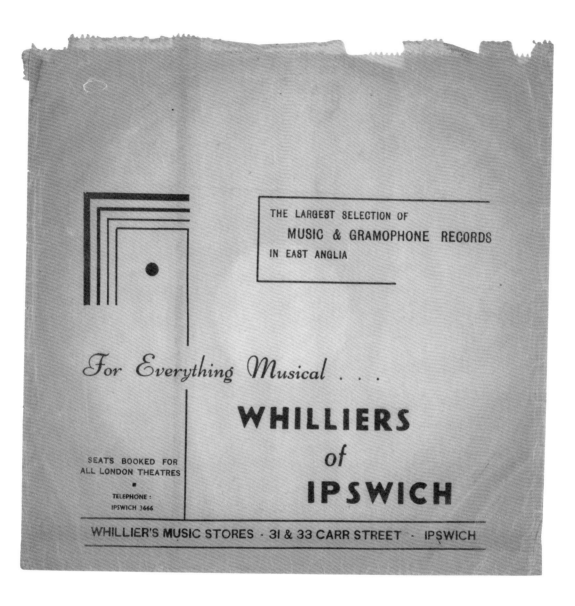

THE LARGEST SELECTION OF
MUSIC & GRAMOPHONE RECORDS
IN EAST ANGLIA

For Everything Musical . . .

WHILLIERS
of
IPSWICH

SEATS BOOKED FOR
ALL LONDON THEATRES

•

TELEPHONE :
IPSWICH 3666

WHILLIER'S MUSIC STORES · 31 & 33 CARR STREET · IPSWICH

WHILLIERS OF IPSWICH

A long-standing gramophone, record and ticket retailer, and the largest stockist of music and records in East Anglia at the time this bag was produced. Sadly, it all came crashing down (literally) as local planners decided Ipswich needed more shopping centres, not lovely old buildings. The resulting Eastgate and Greyfriars shopping centres both ultimately failed, leaving Ipswich a far bleaker place than it might have been, if they'd kept all the old shops.

WH SMITH

Established by Henry Walton Smith and his wife Anna in 1792, the company was inherited by their youngest son, William Henry Smith, in 1812. In 1846, the firm became WH Smith & Son and grew quickly by opening newsstands at stations, capitalising on the railway boom and becoming the first retail chain. In the 1970s, the shops expanded into newer markets such as records. However, the venture into sound was short-lived, as they realised their customers were more interested in their standard fare of stationery, magazines, books and newspapers.

another record from **WHITE & SWALES**

WHITE & SWALES

Founded in 1955, by Noel White and Peter Swales, the shops began by selling sheet music, instruments and records, quickly moving into the burgeoning TV-rentals market and expanding to fifteen branches in total. The design of this blue bag was not exclusive to White & Swales – any shop name could be printed under the words 'another record from'. In 1961, these two influential businessmen saved Altrincham Football Club, which was on the verge of bankruptcy. Both then followed separate paths in football (alongside other business interests), including the chairmanship of Manchester City FC (Swales) and Liverpool FC (White). In 1992, White became one of the founders of the FA Premier League.

ANOTHER RECORD FROM

WHITE & SWALES

WHITE & SWALES LTD.
RECORDS · RADIO · TV · MUSIC

✱ ALTRINCHAM ● STOCKPORT ● WILMSLOW ● STRETFORD ● PARTINGTON

WHITE'S

It's intriguing that this small chain of three shops were all located along the same parade – like a mini empire.

WHITELEYS OF BAYSWATER

One of the first department stores, evolving from a small drapery shop opened in 1863. There is a grand history to all this, but the most interesting part is that they briefly had a little record bar.

WOOLWORTH

A division of the American Woolworth company, this UK retail giant had more than 800 stores before it shut down in 2008. In the UK, they started selling records in the late 1920s. From the 1950s to the 1980s, Woolworth was the UK's biggest music retailer, with a fifth of the chain's income coming from music. Their formula for sonic success was a simple one: to sell affordable musical entertainment to the masses. If they couldn't buy it in, they would make it themselves using their own budget labels – Chevron, Windmill and Embassy (see also Levy's) – that offered up endless compilations and cover versions of current pop hits. The company also distributed the even more dire Stereo Gold Award LPs.

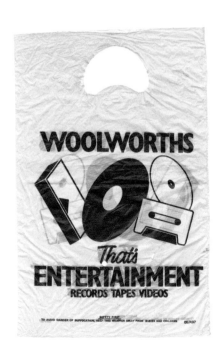

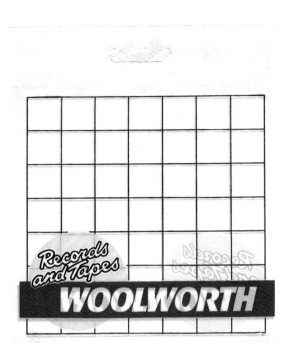

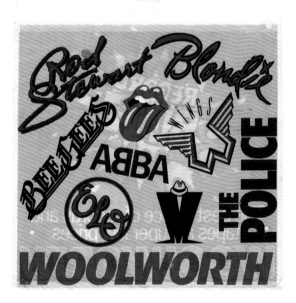

YANKS

Oddly, this long-deceased shop gets mentioned in a few books, the most 'impressive' being penned by Morrissey himself. He describes working for a few months in a basement full of American deletions, all the while having to wear his big overcoat because of the damp conditions. Sounds like heaven to me, but only on days when Morrissey isn't doing his shift.

WORLD

This was one of those shops with a grubby basement where you could spend the whole day getting a bit damp, but unearth all sorts of black gold, each nugget costing about £1.

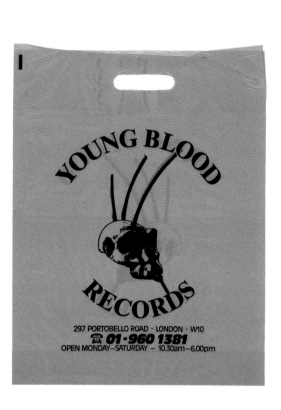

ZIPPO

The final shop in this book is one of the newest, specialising in old vinyl across all genres, interesting imports, funny books and groovy old tees from long-forgotten gigs. Most of their stock is not online, making the shop really worth a visit. The illustration on the printed cotton bag is by Savage Pencil, who has been drawing designs on record bags for decades (see also Parrot and Rough Trade). The shop shares premises with Thurston Moore's Ecstatic Peace Library. So another reason to go. I'm hoping this shop is a sign that the future of record shops in the UK is a bright one.

YOUNG BLOOD

This Portobello Road new wave and punk specialist was situated in the old premises of Shakedown Records, which was previously Musik City, which was Melody Records before that. It is currently a juice bar.

First published in 2022

FUEL Design & Publishing
33 Fournier Street
London E1 6QE

fuel-design.com

All rights reserved.
No part of this publication may be reproduced without
the written permission of the publisher or the copyright
owner.

Scans, research and text by Jonny Trunk
Retouching and colour balancing by Lili Martinez at
Poporo Creative and Derek Collie

Edited by Jonny Trunk, Damon Murray
and Stephen Sorrell

Designed by Murray & Sorrell FUEL
Printed in Belgium

Distributed by Thames & Hudson / D. A. P.
ISBN: 978-1-9162184-8-2

Many bags feature artwork by people we couldn't trace. The
exception was Savage Pencil, and he was fine about us using
his bags in the book, so we hope everyone else will be too.

Special thanks must also go to the following who have
helped massively and generously with this book:

Leon Parker and his British Record Shop Archive
John Spencer at Vintage Hackney Wick
Ben from Ben's Collectors in Guildford
Atlantis Records Hackney
Jake Dragons at Love Vinyl
Colin Rattue
David James at Spitalfields Record Fayre
Mark 'Harry' Harris and Gerri from Red Rhino
Julian Smith at Second Scene Records, Bushey
Simon Gitter for texting me with bag pictures
Geoff from Backtrack / Grammar School Records in Rye
Record Collector magazine for running the wanted bag ads
Ashli at Spillers Records
Paul 'Boots' Lambden
Derek Chapman
Pete Keeley